Home & City Gardener

Home & City Gardener

Roy Hay

octopus

Contents

The Small Garden

First published 1975 by
Octopus Books Limited
59 Grosvenor Street, London W.1.
© 1975 Octopus Books Limited

ISBN 0 7064 0439 4

Produced by Mandarin Publishers Limited,
Westlands Road, Quarry Bay, Hong Kong
Printed in Hong Kong

Growing
Plants
Indoors

Conditions

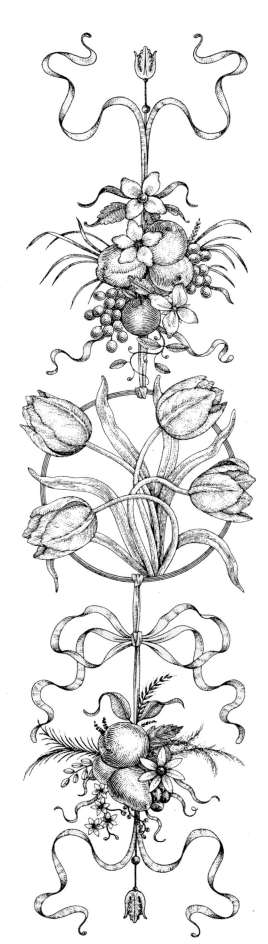

It is only comparatively recently that house plants have become as popular as they now are in city dwellings. At the beginning of this century the potted palm – a *Kentia*, now to be correctly known as *Howea* – was to be seen in many homes, largely among the more affluent, and in most public places. The less affluent contented themselves with a green or gold or silver-striped aspidistra and truly enormous specimens were grown and handed down from generation to generation.

Despite the fact that it is a lovely plant, the aspidistra seems to have taken a back seat in the resurgence of interest in house plants generally. We seldom see one in a florist's shop today or, for that matter, in a home. Its place has been taken by a range of foliage plants all of which require more warmth and few of which will withstand any frost.

While the use of central heating has greatly widened the range of plants that may be grown, it has also brought its problems. The main one, of course, is that the humidity in the air in a centrally heated room is too low for the comfort of many plants. Some, such as the mother-in-law's tongue, *Sansevieria*, the ivies, and the rubber plant, *Ficus elastica*, are not unduly perturbed by the fairly dry atmosphere. Others not so amenable to dry air can be made more comfortable if they are stood on pebbles in shallow trays which are kept filled with water. The moisture evaporating constantly from the water creates a slightly more humid atmosphere – a more congenial microclimate – just around the plants.

Again, several plants may be placed close together in a large container of some kind – an old copper coal bucket or preserving pan, a modern fibre-glass or exfoliated polystyrene 'jardinière' type of container. The pots are plunged in peat which is always kept moist and the evaporating moisture round the plants creates a more favourable atmosphere. If the plants are close enough for the leaves to form a canopy over the container, so much the better – it traps the moist air and stops it rising into the room so fast.

The worst places for plants that need a humid atmosphere, such as the African violets, or saintpaulias, are on a window sill above a radiator or hanging from a bracket on a wall. The warm air rising as it does causes the plant to dry out even more quickly than it would if it were standing on a side table in a room away from the source of heat.

Because we cannot see our plants 'sweating', that is, transpiring moisture through their leaves, we have no idea of how much water they lose in this way. I have not seen any estimates of moisture loss through transpiration of house plants, but to give you some idea of water loss through leaves, a fully grown maize plant in the open can transpire 2 lbs. (0·91 kg.) of water in a day.

Another problem that often arises with central heating is the considerable drop in temperature if, as in many homes, the heating is automatically turned off at night. The heat may be cut off from, say, midnight until 6 in the morning to economize on fuel. This may mean a drop in temperature from something between 21–27°C. (70–80°F.) to something like 13–15°C. (55–60°F), and many plants resent such drastic fluctuations. Even more violent fluctuations of temperature can, of course, occur in houses or apartments that have no central heating.

Then, too, the atmosphere in a living room in the evening may be over-heated and fuggy with tobacco smoke. Flowering plants especially do not like these conditions and it is prudent before a party to remove them to cooler and fresher surroundings. This will help to prolong their flowering.

It must be remembered that the coldest spot in a room on a frosty night is on a window sill between the glass and the curtains. If the curtains in your room shut the plants off from the warmth of the room, bring the pot plants inside the curtains on a cold night.

Then again, there are plants that do not like temperatures much above 15 to 18°C. (60 to 65°F.). The cyclamen is one of these plants, and indeed it reacts strongly and quickly to an over heated and over dry atmosphere. The plant is best – and longest – kept if placed in a cool part of the house, such as the hallway. I grieve to think how many cyclamen, or other pot plants, die within two or three months of being brought into a living room.

More will be said later about the care of cyclamen, but they are plants that do not readily adapt themselves to different growing conditions. It is not only a failure to adapt quickly enough to changed atmospheric conditions that may cause a cyclamen to languish, turn yellow, and drop its buds; it can also be caused by failure on the part of its owner to provide adequate water for the plant to 'live in the style to which it has been accustomed'.

Many pot plants today are grown in greenhouses on sub-irrigation benches. That is, the pots are stood on sand which is always kept moist automatically or they are watered by automatic tubing systems, and the plants draw up just as much water as they require. When you get the plant home from the florist's and you give it whatever amount of water you may think it needs, you may not be giving it as much as it was used to absorbing from its irrigation bench. It will usually soon tell you it is thirsty by drooping, or by losing its fresh bright green colour.

Light is not so great a problem in modern apartments or houses. If anything, you have to be on your guard against certain types of plant receiving too much hot sunlight during the day. Such plants should be kept further back in the room, away from direct sunlight, in summer, and moved nearer the windows in winter. Modern slatted blinds are excellent for windows that receive full sun. They may be adjusted to admit the right amount of sunlight to suit the type of plant being grown.

In old houses, especially in rooms with a north or east aspect, most plants will need to be kept as near the windows as possible.

It is, of course, possible to overcome adverse conditions – of heat, humidity, and even light, by growing plants in containers of one kind or another. Special growing cabinets with heating and lighting are available. Old glass fish tanks – aquaria – glass carboys, even large glass sweet jars may be used to grow various house plants. This aspect of modern cultivation is dealt with in more detail on page 17.

❧ Supplementary Lighting ❧

Some plants, particularly African violets and their many relatives, benefit from some supplementary lighting, either to highlight the plants by means of special spot lights, or to improve their growing conditions. For this purpose, ordinary fluorescent tubes are suitable except in a conservatory or somewhere with a moist atmosphere where waterproof fittings for tubular lighting are essential. Growing cabinets and units fitted with fluorescent tubular lights are also obtainable.

The tubes are usually hung, in reflector housings, about 20 inches (50 cm.) above the base upon which the plants stand, the latter being raised on inverted pots if necessary to be closer for more light. For foliage plants any regular fluorescent tube will do. Flowering plants, however, need more light. For these, use one tube each of wide-spectrum and cool white types or one warm white and one cool white, the latter combination being the less expensive. Usually they are governed by automatic timers to provide light 14 to 16 hours per day.

9

This attractive plant arrangement includes *Philodendron erubescens, Hibiscus rosa-sinensis* hybrid, *Scindapsus aureus, Neoregelia carolinae* 'Tricolor'

Choice of Plants

The choice of pot plants is obviously dictated by a number of factors – the heating arrangements, the amount of daylight available and, very important, the amount of space available. There is also the human factor. Some people have so-called 'green fingers' and grow a wide range of plants indoors with conspicuous success. Yet there are other people who are really best described as 'plant killers'. I know several who admit it quite cheerfully – you would almost think they take a pride in it.

I have never been very convinced by the 'green finger' theory. I am sure that people who have the reputation of being green-fingered have only earned it by years of patient observation and developing a feeling for plants. After all, it is usually 'old Mrs So and So', or 'my old grandmother' who is referred to as having green fingers. You do not often hear people referring to some young person as having the magic touch.

Success with growing anything depends on keen observation, anticipating a plant's needs and devoting sufficient time to the plants. They need to be looked at every day – not that it will be necessary to do something to them every day, but you must get to know and recognize any sign that a plant is not happy, needs more or less water, should be fed or repotted.

Then the amount of space available can to some extent influence the choice of plants. Some of the flowering plants – bulbs such as amaryllis (*Hippeastrum*), fuchsias and others – while charming in flower, are not attractive at other times. One really needs space to accommodate such plants during their off season, where they will not detract from the effect of more attractive plants.

Some plants too, like azaleas, the calamondin orange, *Citrus mitis*, benefit from being stood outdoors in a garden for some weeks in the summer. If you do not have a garden then a balcony or even a window box may be available to accommodate these plants for a time.

Another problem is the care of your plants when you go away for a holiday. Unless you have somebody whom you can trust to water and generally look after the plants intelligently in your absence, it is best to keep to those plants whose needs are simple and which will not suffer greatly from some neglect and maybe erratic watering. There are, of course, automatic watering devices and various techniques which you can adopt to keep plants adequately supplied with water for two or three weeks if necessary, and these are discussed on page 91.

Pot plants roughly fall into two main categories: those which can be grown happily for years in a living room, given favourable conditions and those which will put up with living room conditions for a few months and will then fade away. If a small heated greenhouse or conservatory is available they may be transferred there before they have deteriorated too much. Then, after a period of convalescence, they may return to do another spell of duty in the living room. Indeed, a small greenhouse, even the smallest lean-to, is a splendid investment, and if a lean-to can be constructed so that a window or French doors communicate with it, a delightful feature is added to the home.

A profusion of colour provided by sinningias (gloxinias) and begonias

🌺 Easy Plants 🌺

The following are fairly easy plants to grow in normal living room conditions, always provided their likes and dislikes as regards warmth, light and watering are looked after.

Foliage Plants

Araucaria, Aspidistra, Begonia rex, Chlorophytum, Cissus, Cyperus, Fatshedera, Fatsia, Ferns, *Ficus elastica, Ficus pumila, Hedera* (ivies), *Philodendron, Rhoicissus, Sansevieria, Saxifraga, Scindapsus, Tradescantia.*

Flowering Plants

Begonia semperflorens, Beloperone, Billbergia, Cacti, *Campanula isophylla, Clivia, Epiphyllum, Fuchsia, Hippeastrum, Impatiens, Pelargonium, Primula obconica, Schlumbergera, Streptocarpus.*

🌺 Foliage Plants 🌺

Broadly speaking the foliage plants are the easiest to keep growing happily in the home. They fall into three main categories, those which make shapely plants like *Sansevieria, Fatshedera* and the like; the climbing plants like ivies, *Cissus, Philodendron* and *Scindapsus,* and the trailing plants suitable for hanging baskets and for hanging down over the side of large containers, such as *Tradescantia, Ficus pumila* and *Gynura sarmentosa.* The latter two may be considered together because several, like the ivies, *Ficus pumila* and *Cissus,* can be grown either up a supporting framework or hanging down.

🌺 Climbing and Trailing Plants 🌺

There is a good range of climbers which can be grown up a trellis to form a natural division to a room. The plants are best grown in pots plunged in peat within the container rather than being planted direct in the containers.

Climbers too may be grown around a wigwam of canes or a wire framework in a variety of shapes. This type of support is very popular with climbing flowers such as *Hoya carnosa.*

Climbing Plants

Cissus, Ficus, Hedera, Hoya, Monstera, Philodendron, Rhoicissus, Scindapsus, Thunbergia alata.

Trailing Plants

Trailing plants play an important part in any plant arrangement and, indeed, a single trailer can be most attractive on its own. Most of the trailers are easily propagated by cuttings and so one can use them fairly generously to hide, or in many cases to enhance, a container.
Asparagus, Cissus, Ficus, Gynura, Tradescantia, Zebrina.

🌺 Flowering and Fruiting Plants 🌺

Flowering plants and those grown for their ornamental fruits are generally regarded as more difficult to accommodate happily in the home than foliage plants. Some like hydrangeas really need a period standing outdoors in semi-shade after flowering. Others like saintpaulias do not like temperatures that fall below 10°C (50°F.) at night and cyclamen are really happiest when this temperature is kept between 10–13°C. (50–55°F.); it can rise higher but the plants will not last so long in flower. The flowering plants described on pp. 31–34 may be reasonably expected to last a year or two, some for many years. Of the fruiting plants mentioned, *Citrus mitis*, the calamondin orange, will probably last longest in the home. It will make a bush about 2 feet (60 cm.) high and wide. It produces small, rather bitter, oranges about the size of a plum. The capsicums are usually grown as annuals and discarded after they have fruited; the winter cherry, *Solanum capsicastrum* is usually treated likewise. It can be trimmed back in March however, repotted and kept for another year.

 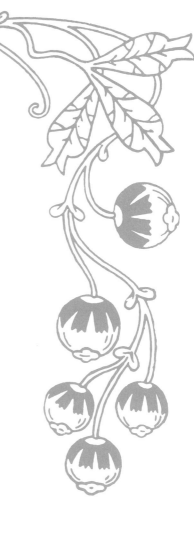

Bulbs

Bulbs are among the most rewarding of plants to grow indoors, and of course outdoors as well. Nature has done 90 per cent of the work for us because a bulb contains in embryo the already formed leaves, stem and flower, and all we have to do is provide the right conditions for the bulb to grow and blossom.

Bulbs indoors fall into two categories – those that may be grown in pots for years, like the *Hippeastrum* or amaryllis, and those which we grow in pots or bowls to flower indoors once and then to be planted out in the garden or discarded.

Of the bulbs that we grow in bowls or pots there is the possibility of growing prepared bulbs that will flower for Christmas or very early in the new year. Daffodils and tulips are given special pre-cooling treatment by the bulb growers to encourage them to flower earlier than normal and hyacinths are also treated – they are given heat treatment in fact – to flower easily by Christmas. Then of course there is a great range of bulbs beside the daffodils, hyacinths and tulips, which can be grown in pots indoors – scillas, muscari, ranunculus, crocuses, tritonias, ixias, sparaxis, and even chionodoxas.

Bulbs such as those of hippeastrums which are to be grown in the same pot for years need to be potted originally in a fairly good loam-based potting soil. If this is not available, one of the peat-based mixtures may be used.

For those bulbs to be grown only for flowering once indoors and then to be planted out in the garden a special bulb fibre based on peat with charcoal and crushed shell added to keep the mixture sweet, is the best type of medium to use. These bulbs may be grown in pots with a drainage hole, or in bowls without drainage. Obviously watering is more tricky in bowls without drainage. It is necessary to water regularly to keep the peat fibre always moist as it is very difficult to wet again if it is allowed to dry out. Do make sure that there is no surplus water lying at the bottom of the bowl. Put your hand over the bulbs and the fibre to keep them in place, and tip the bowl gently on its side to allow surplus water to drain out.

It is also important never to allow water to touch the developing bud of a hyacinth because if this happens it is quite likely that a number of the little florets on the spike will turn brown and fail to develop.

Planting Bulbs

See that the potting mix is just moist but not too wet – a little moisture should escape between your fingers if you squeeze a handful. Spread a layer of the mix on the bottom of the bowl or pot and then gently place the bulbs in contact with the fibre, but do not firm them down too much. Fill up the container with more fibre so that the noses of the bulbs are just visible above the top of the mix.

A most imposing display can be obtained by planting 2 layers of tulips, or daffodils, in an 8–10 inch (20–25 cm.) pot. The technique here is to half-fill the pot with the fibre or peat-based mixture and then place 5 double-nosed daffodil bulbs, or 8–10 tulips on the mixture half way up the pot. Add more mix and place another layer of daffodils, say 7 daffodil bulbs, or another 8 or 9 tulip bulbs, on top. The lower bulbs will grow up between the uppermost ones and a massive display of blooms is the result.

It is important to keep bulbs in pots or bowls as cool as possible. It is preferable also to keep them in the dark until they are well rooted, but this is not necessary. You can place them in black plastic bags in a cupboard or somewhere until they are showing signs of growth. They may then be brought out into the warmth and light gradually. The essential is to try and keep them at a temperature of about 4–7°C. (40–45°F.) for 8 to 10 weeks after planting to encourage good root development.

When the daffodils or tulips have made about 2 inches (5 cm.) of growth they should be ready to be brought into a warm room. Do not bring hyacinths into the warmth until the bud is well clear of the neck of the bulb.

When you do bring bulbs into the warmth accustom them to the light gradually. Put them fairly well back in the room for a few days until they become green because the stems will be rather pale and yellow after being brought out of the dark, and gradually move them towards the light. Turn the bowl every day so the plants do not draw too much towards the light.

Remember that the window sill can be the coldest place in the house at night. All pot plants, and especially bulbs, should be brought into the room before the curtains are drawn on a cold night.

When bulbs have finished flowering place them in some odd corner if possible, or even outside on a balcony or in the garden if the weather is warm enough. Continue to water them until the foliage dies down if it is not possible to plant them out. Alternatively, if they can be planted in the ground, tip them out of their bowl and plant as soon as flowering is over.

Bulbs that have once been forced in pots or bowls cannot be used a second time for this purpose. With the probable exception of tulips which must be looked upon as expendable, most bulbs will flower again in the garden, but they may take a year or more to recover from their forcing.

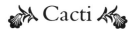 Cacti

Cacti and other succulent plants are excellent for growing in the home as most of them will survive short periods of neglect better than most house plants. Those described on page 34 are fairly easy to grow in the home and should flower regularly.

Herbs

If there is room for a box or a few pots in a sunny window it is possible to grow an interesting range of herbs indoors. Some, such as sage and rosemary, need frequent pinching to stop them from becoming too large. They need to be replaced by young plants every year or so. Normal snipping or pinching of leaves or shoots as required for culinary use is usually sufficient to keep the plants bushy and compact. It is of course easily possible to clip them too hard and this temptation must be avoided. It is probably best to grow the different herbs in separate pots and plunge them in peat in a box or container. If planted direct in a box or trough some of the more invasive herbs like mint may be too rampant for the others.

Grow them in any normal potting mixture and feed with liquid fertilizer as directed by the manufacturers. The following are worth growing indoors:

Balm, a perennial which may be kept to a low bush by frequent pinching of the shoots. Propagate by division.

Basil, an annual raised from seed sown in March. Pinch shoots regularly to keep the plant to about 12 inches (30 cm.) high.

Cactus dish garden

Bay, a small bay tree may be grown in a pot for a number of years until it becomes too big. Propagate by cuttings.

Chives, which grow well in containers in sun or partial shade if given a rest before forcing. Propagate by division.

Marjoram, a dwarf bushy hardy perennial much used in 'bouquets garnis', stuffings and stews. The common marjoram and the sweet marjoram prefer a sunny aspect. Propagate by seed or cuttings.

Mint, best kept in a box on its own as it is very invasive. There are several kinds of mint but spearmint is probably the best for a window box. Mint will grow in sun or partial shade. Cut the plants down in October. Some pieces of root may be placed in a box or pot of soil and brought indoors to provide fresh leaves in winter. Propagate by division.

Parsley, this also will grow in sun or partial shade. Seeds are sown in March or April. Thin the seedlings as soon as they are large enough to handle, leaving the plants 6 inches (15 cm.) apart. Cover them with a glass or plastic cloche in the winter.

Rosemary, like sage will make a large bush but can be kept small and bushy by regularly pinching the young shoots. Propagate by cuttings.

Sage, must be trimmed frequently to keep it bushy and about 2 feet (60 cm.) high. It will grow in sun or partial shade. Propagate by cuttings.

Tarragon, pinch growth regularly to keep the plant to about 12–18 inches (30–45 cm.) high. Propagate by division.

Thyme, there are several types of thyme, including varieties with gold or silver variegated foliage. Propagate by cuttings.

Mustard and cress, while they cannot be classified as herbs, may be grown very easily indoors in full light on pads of cotton wool, flannel or old sacking or in a seed sowing mixture. Sow cress 3 days before the mustard or rape seed. They will both be ready 11–14 days after sowing the cress.

Plants from Pips

You can have a certain amount of fun by growing plants from kitchen scraps such as date, peach or avocado stones, orange and lemon pips, and tops of pineapples. Many of these plants can eventually grow too big for an indoor situation but will meanwhile, however, give much pleasure.

An amusing and cheap way of obtaining greenery is to slice off the top of root vegetables such as carrots, beetroot and turnips. Remove any old or broken leaves, and stand the flat base of the sliced off part in a tray with an inch or two of pebbles and fill with water. Keep the tray full of water and new growths will appear giving fresh foliage for months.

There are several ways of germinating seeds from orange, grapefruit, lemons, apples and pears. One is to sow them in a pot of peat kept moist in a plastic bag. Another is to put them between two thick paper napkins and keep these always moist. The seeds should germinate in about a month, and the seedlings can then be potted singly in small pots.

To germinate an avocado stone, pierce it with several toothpicks or cocktail sticks, and suspend it over a jar or tumbler of water. The pointed end should be uppermost, the other end constantly in the water. When roots appear, pot the stone in an 8 inch pot. The growths need to be pinched to promote side shoots, and these too are pinched or stopped in turn to promote bushy growth.

Peach, apricot or plum stones should be cracked and sown in sand or peat, and kept moist. They may take several months to germinate.

The trick with a pineapple top, after cutting off the leaves and a slice of the fruit, is to run a hot iron over the flesh very quickly to seal it. Otherwise the flesh will rot. Plant it in a pot of gritty soil and water it very sparingly.

15

Displaying Plants

Use of Plants in Containers, Tubs and Jardinières

The possible combinations of pot plants in containers such as tubs, jardinières, plastic or wooden troughs, old coal buckets, preserving pans and other containers are limitless. The easiest to maintain are those composed entirely of foliage plants which can remain in their containers for months at a time needing only the normal maintenance and eventually perhaps some pruning, or thinning out as plants grow too large for the space available.

Such arrangements of foliage plants need not be dull if gold and silver variegated plants such as ivies are planted together with say the purple-leaved *Gynura sarmentosa*, the green and purple *Zebrina* and say a *Codiaeum* (croton) with yellow or variegated leaves. In all containers of any size it is normal to place a trailing plant or two such as an ivy, a *Tradescantia* or a fig such as *Ficus pumila* to hang down the side of the container. Then an upright *Dizygotheca* with its bronzy foliage, a *Sansevieria*, a *Begonia rex*, or a combination of these plants would make an attractive display.

If desired, a basic planting of green, variegated or coloured foliage plants can be enlivened by the addition of one or more flowering pot plants – an azalea or cyclamen in winter, a primula, gloxinia, geranium or fuchsia at other times.

A pot of daffodils, tulips or hyacinths in a container with, grouped around it some *Pteris* or *Nephrolepis* ferns, or rex begonias is most attractive. Again a *Chlorophytum* with its yellow and green-striped leaves contrasts well with *Fatshedera*, ivies and perhaps a *Monstera* plant.

Pot et fleurs

We have borrowed from the French this descriptive phrase to cover a skilful association of foliage plants in pots and cut flowers arranged in concealed vases or jars of water.

There is much to be said for this technique. The foliage plants form the basis of the arrangement which is enlivened by the cut flowers – different flowers in the different seasons – and you do not become bored with the foliage plants.

It is also economical of flowers as, say, 5 daffodils or tulips or 3 or 4 chrysanthemums make a colourful contrast with the foliage plants.

Bottle Gardens

A terrarium is basically a glass container that is planted with a carefully chosen selection of plants to achieve a balanced environment. The plants absorb moisture from the soil, transpire it through their leaves and after it has condensed take it in again from the soil. Naturally this calls for careful management – seeing that the soil is kept only moist, not wet and that the top of the container is kept in position unless water condenses and fogs the inside of the glass. When this happens it is left partially open at night to allow some ventilation.

With bottles of varying sizes up to the large glass carboys that were used for transporting chemicals, now alas almost collector's items, begin by depositing a layer of an inch or so (a few cm.) of pea gravel on the bottom. This is then covered with 3–4 inches of potting mix. This has to be poured in dry and it is important that the inside of the glass is dry as if by chance soil sticks to wet glass as you are pouring it in it is difficult to clean it off.

Unless the bottle, carboy or other glass container – old fish tank or specially made glass case – is open at the top or has an opening through which a small hand can pass, you have to make a few primitive tools. An old kitchen fork with the prongs bent at right angles to the handles or an old tea spoon may be tied to a cane. These implements enable you to dig a little hole in the planting mixture and after placing a plant in it to draw the soil up to cover the roots. It is possible to lower the plant into place by holding it between 2 pieces of cane. A thread reel on the end of a cane is useful for tamping or firming the soil gently. When the plants are all in place spread a layer of small gravel or stone chippings over the planting mixture after watering it well.

Depending on the size of the bottle or other receptacle a choice of plants for terrariums may be made from the following:
Cryptanthus, Fittonia, Ferns, *Hedera* (ivies), Mosses, *Peperomia, Pilea, Saintpaulia, Saxifraga, Sedum, Tradescantia, Zebrina.* Cacti

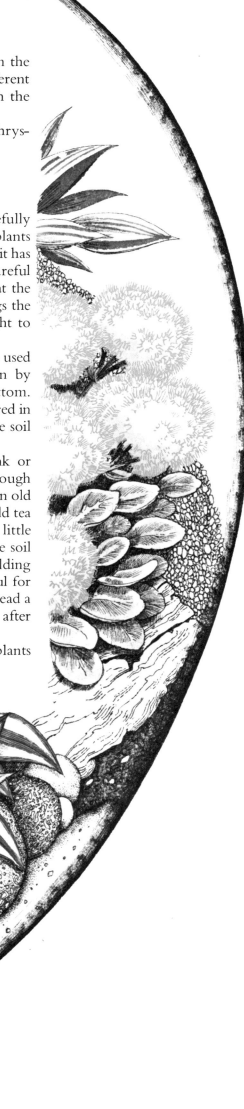

❧ Hanging Baskets ❧

The different types of hanging baskets and pots and how to plant in them are described on page 36 where we are considering these containers for use outdoors.

Indoors the plastic pot with a 'built-in' saucer at the base is convenient as with care you can water it without having to take it out and stand it over a basin or sink. Failing this type, or if the plastic bowl is considered unsightly even when partially hidden by trailing plants you may use an open wire or metal type of basket.

A layer of sphagnum moss is packed round the inside of the basket and the pots are bedded in more moss. This type of basket of course needs more careful and frequent watering than the solid plastic bowl type.

Many lovely combinations of plants may be arranged in a hanging pot or basket. Quite a simple display may be made from 4–5 different varieties of ivy – say one of the crested leaf types, a small green variety and both a silver and gold variegated form. One could be trained to grow up over one or two short sticks and the others allowed to hang down.

Alternatively you could combine a bush-type fuchsia with some trailing plants; an ivy-leaved geranium hanging down with an upright begonia and one or two trailing ivies or tradescantias form a colourful basket.

Plants for Hanging Baskets

Asparagus, Begonia, Campanula isophylla, Chlorophytum, Cissus, Ficus pumila, Ficus repens, Fuchsia, Gynura, Hedera (ivy), *Impatiens, Pelargonium* (geranium), *Saxifraga stolonifera* (syn. *S. sarmentosa*), *Streptocarpus, Schlumbergera, Tradescantia, Zebrina.*

❧ Miniature Gardens ❧

Great pleasure may be had from miniature gardens indoors and of course outdoors too.

Almost any kind of bowl, tray, trough or similar container is suitable for making a miniature garden provided it has at least one drainage hole in the base. It means of course that the garden must be on a tray of some kind to protect furniture from moisture draining out from the container.

The round or square earthenware pans or 'half pots' as they are known in the flower pot business are excellent as they have adequate drainage holes. Some people do not like the 'flower pot red' or terracotta colouring but you can always paint the outside with a stone-coloured cement wash if desired.

Cover the drainage hole or holes with one or two pieces of broken flower pot or china, then cover the base of the container with a layer of an inch or so of pebbles or broken flower pot. On top of the pebbles place a layer of peat and then fill the container to about two-thirds of its depth with preferably a loam-based potting mix. If this is not available fill it with a peat-based compost, in which case it is not necessary to put the layer of peat over the pebbles. Place one or two pieces of rock so that they are partially submerged and then 'landscape' the surface soil so that it undulates gently.

One or two true dwarf conifers, *Saxifraga stolonifera* or other low growing house plants may then be placed in position.

Alternatively a small garden may be made entirely of cacti – a desert garden. For this a sandy soil and plenty of drainage material in the bottom of the container are necessary. Garden shops often sell a soil mixture especially for cacti.

All the plants mentioned on page 17 for bottle gardens may of course be grown in miniature gardens.

Various ferns and ivy have been used to great
effect in these hanging baskets

Propagation

There are several ways of raising house plants, or of increasing your stock. The most commonly practised is rooting cuttings, usually, but not exclusively, of the foliage plants. Propagation by leaf cuttings is an easy way of increasing some plants like begonias and African violets.

Plants like sansevierias, aspidistras and clivias may be increased by division of the root when it has made a sufficient number of growths.

Many house plants grown for their flowers, and also a number of foliage plants are raised from seed.

A fourth way of increasing your stock is to detach and plant the small plantlets which are produced on the parent plants. The thousand mothers, or pig-a-back plant, *Tolmiea menziesii*, and *Chlorophytum elatum* are propagated in this way.

Air layering is sometimes practised for rooting a shoot of a large shrubby plant like a *Ficus* or rubber plant.

❧ Cuttings ❧

Cuttings may be taken from either the stem or the leaf of the plant. Many cuttings will not root unless grown in a warm and humid atmosphere. This may be artificially provided by using a propagating case.

You can buy plastic seed trays which have dome-like covers. Some of the plastic covers have adjustable ventilators set in the top of the cover. You can also buy propagating cases with electric heating capable of maintaining temperatures of 21–27°C. (70–80°F.) which are desirable for raising seeds of certain types of tropical plants. For most cuttings, however, ordinary room temperatures of around 21°C (70°F) are satisfactory.

An improvised propagator can be made by filling either a box or a large flower pot with the cutting medium and then bending 4 pieces of wire into a rough half circle and pushing the ends into the pot. After the cuttings have been inserted in the potting mix, drape thin clear plastic over the wires and tie it round the pot just below the rim.

Most stem cuttings consist of young unflowered shoots about 3–4 inches (7·5–10 cm.) long. The lowest pair of leaves is removed and a clean cut is made with a sharp knife or a razor blade just below the node or joint where the lower leaves were removed. This is the type of cutting made from plants of *Pelargonium* (geranium), *Hydrangea*, *Fuchsia*, *Tradescantia*, *Cissus* and similar plants.

The prepared shoots are inserted in a mixture of peat and really coarse sand or, as some call it, grit. The fine sticky yellow sand is not good for this purpose as the object of mixing the sand with the peat is to help drainage and to keep the mixture sweet. For most cuttings equal parts by bulk of moist peat and sand is a suitable mixture. Or you can buy proprietary peat-based cuttings mixtures. There are also peat-based mixtures which are suitable for seed sowing, rooting cuttings and for potting.

Some people use a 'hormone' type of rooting compound to hasten rooting. The base of the cutting is dipped in the powder before it is inserted in the rooting medium. Some rooting compounds contain a fungicide such as captan which helps to prevent the cutting from rotting at the base. Bruising of the base of the cutting, as often happens if they are cut with secateurs, may encourage rotting. For this reason always use a sharp knife or a razor blade.

Make sure the cutting mixture is nicely moist. Insert the cuttings around the inner edge of the flower pot, making a hole with a pencil deep enough to

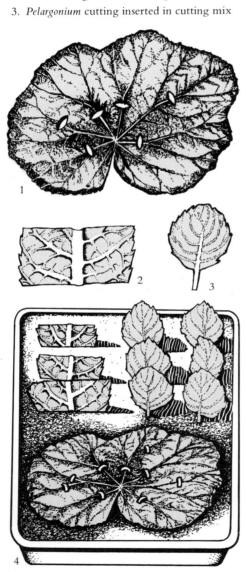

1. Stem cutting of a *Hydrangea*
2. Stem cutting of a zonal *Pelargonium*
3. *Pelargonium* cutting inserted in cutting mix

1. A *Begonia* leaf with cuts made through the veins
2. Sections of a *Streptocarpus* leaf
3. A *Saintpaulia* leaf
4. The leaves appropriately placed in the cutting medium

take the bottom 2 inches (5 cm.) or so of the cutting. Do not make the hole too deep – the base of the cutting should rest on the soil at the bottom of the hole.

When the cuttings have been inserted, and the plastic cover put in place, stand the pot in a light place but out of direct sunshine.

A pot is really the best receptacle for rooting a small number of cuttings. If a large number is required use a seed box, but do not cram the cuttings in too close together – they should not touch each other. As soon as the cuttings have rooted, put them singly in small pots – 3 inch (7·5 cm.) diameter is a good size for the first potting.

Short shoots, about 4 inches (10 cm.) long, of some foliage plants such as ivy and *Impatiens* (busy lizzie) will produce roots if the stems are inserted for about 2 inches (5 cm.) of their length in water. When they have produced roots an inch (about 2·5 cm.) or so in length they may be inserted carefully in a small pot – 3 inch (7·5 cm.) diameter – of potting soil.

Leaf Cuttings

A number of plants, notably *Saintpaulia*, *Streptocarpus* and *Begonia* may be propagated by leaf cuttings. With *Saintpaulia*, the African violet, a leaf with a length of stem is used, and the bottom inch or so of stem is inserted in the cutting medium. African violet leaves will also make roots if the bottom inch or so of stem is inserted in water. *Streptocarpus* leaves are cut right across horizontally in sections about 1–2 inches (2·5–5 cm.) wide. These are inserted in the soil vertically.

Leaves of *Begonia rex* and similar foliage forms may be treated in different ways. A whole leaf may be laid on the surface of the cutting medium, and cuts made through the veins at a distance of about 2 inches (5 cm.) apart with a razor blade or a sharp knife. Small stones are placed at intervals on the leaf, or pegs of bent wire are used, to keep the cut surfaces in contact with the soil.

Alternatively small pieces of leaf about the size of a large postage stamp, each piece containing a section of a vein, may be laid on the rooting medium or inserted in it to half their depth vertically. The cuttings, leaves or leaf sections must be kept moist and in a temperature of 18–24°C. (65–75°F.). They will root best if kept in a propagating case or in a box covered with a sheet of glass or plastic film.

Air Layering

This is a favourite method of propagating certain types of plant with a woody stem, such as the rubber plant, *Ficus elastica*, or cordylines.

At a point, say 2 feet (60 cm.) below the top of the shoot, make an upward slit in the stem about 1–1½ inches (2·5–4 cm.) long. Wedge the slit open with a sliver of wood. Additionally, if desired, remove a narrow circle of bark about ½ an inch (1·3 cm.) wide round the stem just above the slit. Dust this area liberally with rooting compound. Then wrap thin plastic film round the stem, tying it below the slit. The film should be wide enough and over-lapping so that it forms a kind of cylindrical 'bag' over the cut part. Fill this container with moist sphagnum moss or peat, and then tie it to the stem above the cut. In about 10 weeks roots should grow from the wounded area, and the stem may then be severed from the parent plant and the new plant potted carefully, taking care not to damage the roots.

Plantlets

Several plants we may grow in the home produce tiny plantlets on their leaves, or on stems or stolons. These little plantlets may be detached carefully

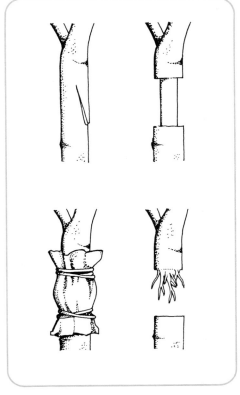

Air layering

21

and rooted in a pot or box of cutting medium. Some plantlets, such as those that appear on stems produced on plants of *Chlorophytum elatum*, may be left until they are say 2 inches (5 cm.) high before they are detached. Those produced at the top of the leaf stalk on *Tolmiea menziesii* are detached as soon as they are large enough to handle.

Another plant that produces small plantlets is *Saxifraga stolonifera* (*S. sarmentosa*), commonly known as mother of thousands, Aaron's beard, roving sailor or strawberry geranium. The red creeping stems or stolons are produced from the heart of the plant, and these bear the young plantlets which root easily.

A succulent plant easy to grow in the home is *Bryophyllum daigremontianum*. It produces many tiny plantlets around the edges of the leaves. These may be detached when they are quite small – $\frac{1}{4}$–$\frac{1}{2}$ inch (0·64–1·3 cm.) across, and 'sown' or scattered on the cutting or seed sowing mix in a pot, and kept warm and moist. They root very easily.

Division

A few plants are propagated by division of the crowns, or by separating 'offset' shoots as in sansevierias. Prise the soil away from the ball of soil and loosen the roots as much as possible. Then with a sharp knife separate and sever where necessary young well rooted pieces of the old plant. Pot these separately.

Seeds

Many flowering plants such as *Cyclamen*, *Clivia*, *Impatiens* and *Begonia* are easily raised from seed provided one has the space on a window sill or on a bench near a window. Many foliage plants too may be raised from seeds – *Coleus*, *Ficus*, *Pilea* and *Grevillea* among them.

It is also possible to raise young plants from date and peach stones, orange and lemon pips, and the seed of the avocado pear (see page 15). This gives a certain amount of interest and pleasure, but eventually the plants become too large for a living room and have to be discarded.

As with propagation by cuttings, no elaborate equipment is necessary although it helps to have a heated propagating case that can be kept at a temperature of 21–27°C. (70–80°F.). Failing this, a pot or box with a plastic cover as described on p. 20 may be stood near a radiator or in another warm situation to maintain a steady degree of heat. It is not necessary to exclude light from the seed pot or box. The only seed I know which must have darkness for germination is *Nigella*, the love in a mist, which is never germinated indoors or in a greenhouse. The reason why gardeners used to cover their seed pots or boxes with brown paper was to keep them shaded from strong sun and from drying out unnecessarily. Naturally, as soon as the seeds are seen to have germinated, they must be brought into the light.

Fill the pot or box with a seed sowing mixture, either one based on loam, or a peat-based mix. Level it very gently by pressing a flat board on the surface, but on no account consolidate the mixture – just make an even level surface. Sow the seeds very thinly. With fine seeds it helps to mix them with fine dry sand before sowing. Just cover the seed with fine sifted soil or fine sand.

When the seedlings have opened 2 leaves, prick them off – that is, transplant them into another box, or singly into very small 1–2 inch (2·5–5 cm.) diameter pots. Later on they will be transferred to 3–3½ inch (7·5–9 cm.) pots in which they should pass their first year or 18 months. After seedlings have been pricked off shade them from strong light, and of course see that they

This effective room-divider uses *Neoregelia carolinae* 'Tricolor', *Philodendron erubescens*, *Sansevieria trifasciata* 'Laurentii', *Dracaena deremensis*, *Vriesea splendens*, *Cyperus alternifolius*, *Ficus elastica* 'Doescheri', *Schefflera actinophylla*, *Scindapsus aureus*

never dry out.

Cactus seeds are often sold as a mixture of as many as a dozen species or varieties. These often germinate over a long period – months even. So, as the seedlings appear, carefully remove them, using the tip of a penknife blade, as they become large enough, and pot them singly in small pots.

The flat seeds of the attractive foliage plant *Grevillea robusta* germinate best if they are inserted in the soil edgewise.

Care of Plants

Success with house plants depends on several factors. One is the maintenance of temperatures within the upper and lower ranges that the plants being grown will tolerate. We must accept that if we cannot do this, some plants will sulk and dwindle away and we end up, as we should probably have begun, by trying to find plants to fit their surroundings rather than by trying to make the surroundings fit the plants.

❧ Watering ❧

More plants are killed by overwatering than by being kept too dry. Here are some points to remember:

The larger the leaf area the more water the plant will transpire through the leaves.

The warmer the atmosphere the more water the leaves will transpire. Plants will use more water in spring and summer when they are in active growth than in winter when growth is not so active.

Plants standing on their own with dry warm air circulating freely around them will dry out more quickly than several plunged together in a container filled with moist peat.

Plants in clay pots will need watering more often than those in plastic pots as water evaporates through the sides of a clay pot but not through plastic. If, therefore, you have several plants in a jardinière or other container, do not mix clay and plastic pots. Watering will be easier if you have all clay or all plastic pots.

Many plants today are grown in peat-based mixes. If these are allowed to dry out it is very difficult to wet the mix again by pouring water into the top of the pot. This applies, but to a lesser extent, to loam-based mixtures. The soil ball shrinks, leaving a small gap between it and the pot wall. You pour in water, but most of it runs down through this gap and out at the bottom. With either type of mix, but essentially with the peat-based ones, it is best to plunge the pot in a basin or bucket of tepid water. When bubbles stop coming to the surface the soil will have absorbed enough water.

It is not possible to say that you should apply water once a week, every 2 or 3 days, or according to any preconceived programme. You should apply water when the plants need it, and just before they tell you they are thirsty by allowing their leaves to droop. It does not matter very much if the leaves do flag a little now and then, but it is better to see that plants do not suffer from want of water.

If you have plants in a container or a cache-pot, there should be a layer of peat, sand or pebbles at the bottom so that if surplus water drains through the pot it will not be standing in a pool of water. Individual pots are often stood in a saucer or some kind of deepish tray to protect the surface of furniture or a window sill. Again, do not let such trays fill with water. It is better to fill the tray with pebbles so that the base of the pot is not standing in a pool of water.

If you look at your plants frequently – every day or two – you will soon get to know when they need water. Simply by lifting a pot you will be able to tell whether it feels light and therefore needs water. If you tap a clay pot with

To retain moisture, group several pots together in a container filled with moist peat.

Stand the pot on pebbles and not directly in water

your knuckle it will ring hollow if the soil mixture is dry, but there will be a dull thud if it is wet.

As a general rule it is best to wait until a plant needs a good watering, and to give it plenty, allowing surplus water to drain away.

Some plants need more careful watering than others. Begonias, for example, do not like water on their leaves in hot sunshine – the little globules of water act as a lens and scorching of the leaves can occur. Cyclamen, when flower buds are present, should be watered from below, by standing the pot in water so that it comes half way up the pot. The soil mix will eventually soak up water until it is wet again. If you do water from above take care not to allow water to come into contact with the small flower buds on top of the corm since they may rot.

As I said before, a plant will tell you if it is thirsty by flagging, and no great harm will be done. But by the time a plant tells you it has had too much water for too long, by rotting at the base or by its leaves turning yellow, becoming spotted, or by buds or leaves dropping off, it is often too late to do much about it. Obviously a much drier regime is indicated, and on no account should a sickly plant be fed with liquid fertilizer.

It can happen, especially in winter and if plants are being kept in rather low temperatures, that the leaves may droop causing you to think the plants are dry. But they may flag because they are too wet, and if you give them more water you only make them more unhappy.

Feeding

To keep pot plants growing happily the roots obviously must be able to absorb adequate supplies of food. This they do by absorbing the plant nutrients in solution – they cannot take in solid food. Hence another reason for seeing that plants get all the water they need.

When you buy a pot plant, or if you propagate your own using, usually, a 3–4 inch (7·5–10 cm.) diameter pot for their first potting, they can generally be kept in this size pot for a year. Then if the ball of soil mix is permeated by roots and these are wrapped thickly round the outside of the ball, the plant needs repotting. This is explained in more detail on page 26.

When a plant has rooted nicely into its mix, no matter what size of pot, after 2–3 months it responds to regular feeding. Plants are fed during their growing season – spring to autumn, March to October, and not during the winter when growth is not active.

There are many proprietary fertilizers specially formulated for pot plants, and these should be applied according to the maker's instructions. With some concentrated liquid fertilizers it is usual to add a few drops to the can of water each time you water your plants. With others, you see that the soil is moist, not saturated, and then you apply a dose of the diluted plant food. Never apply fertilizer to dry soil.

With some fertilizers it often pays to apply the liquid at half the recommended strength and twice as often as the makers suggest. Many plants seem to appreciate this 'little and often' treatment.

There are also solid fertilizers which can be sprinkled on the surface of the soil, but these have to be watered in anyway, so it is really more convenient to apply a liquid fertilizer in the first place.

Foliar feeding – that is, applying the fertilizers by spraying it on the leaves of plants is becoming very popular. There are several foliar feeds containing the basic plant foods as well as a number of trace elements which plants need. A fine spraying with a foliar feed now and then stimulates root action and improves the colour of the foliage. Do not, however, apply foliar feeds to plants standing in full sun.

Newly repotted plant showing original soil ball in larger pot of fresh potting mix, see following page.

25

Repotting

When a plant has made a large amount of root growth it needs moving into a larger pot. To find out if a plant needs repotting, put your hand over the top of the ball of soil with your fingers either side of the plant, invert the pot, and tap the edge smartly on the top of a table or shelf. The plant should come cleanly out of the pot. If the roots are virtually covering the outside of the ball then the plant needs repotting.

Usually when a plant needs repotting it is moved into a pot an inch or so larger all round – from a $3\frac{1}{2}$ inch (9 cm.) pot to a 5 inch (13 cm) pot, and so on. Do not 'overpot' – that is, do not put a plant in a pot unnecessarily large. If there is too great a volume of soil it may become sour before the plant roots have penetrated it thoroughly.

Once you have decided that a plant needs repotting, and which size pot you are going to use, remove the top inch or so (a few cm.) of soil from the top of the soil ball. If the ball is very thickly encased in roots, press the sides of the ball firmly to loosen some of the roots. If the plant has been in a clay pot there will probably be embedded in the base of the soil ball, one or more pieces of 'crock' or broken pot which were put in to ensure good drainage. Remove these and tease out the roots at the base.

If you are going to put the plant into another clay pot then 'crock' it by placing a large piece of broken pot over the drainage hole and one or two small pieces on top of this. It is not necessary to crock plastic pots as the drainage holes are usually more numerous and smaller so that there is no danger of soil washing out through the bottom of the pot.

Whether you use clay or plastic pots, make sure that they are scrupulously clean. Soak them in water with household detergent and brush off all dirt. Soak new clay pots thoroughly in clear water before use.

After placing the crocks if a clay pot is used, put a layer of potting mix in the bottom of the pot. Make the layer thick enough so that the top of the ball of soil is about an inch below the level of the pot rim. Then fill the space between the old soil ball and the new pot with potting mix, working it in with a wooden label or with fingers. Cover the top of the old ball with mix, but allow about $\frac{1}{2}$–$\frac{3}{4}$ inch (1·3–2 cm.) between the top of the mix and the pot rim to make watering easy. Usually if you fill the pot with water this is all the plant requires at that particular watering.

Firm loam-based mixes gently, but do not firm peat-based composts. Just tap the pot smartly on the bench to settle the mix; the necessary watering in will consolidate the mix sufficiently. If peat composts are firmed they will become waterlogged and plants will rot.

Always water newly potted or repotted plants and keep them in a warm spot, but shaded from the sun for a few days until they have settled into the new mix.

Diseases and Pests

In many cases diseases are caused, or aggravated by unsatisfactory conditions. Be vigilant for the first signs of trouble, and check for possible causes – watering, irregular temperatures, draughts, too dry an atmosphere, fumes, poor light conditions, starvation or actual presence of pests.

It is very difficult to cure a disease. The most one can do is to try to provide conditions which will not encourage the incidence and spread of disease, see pages 8–9. In most cases rotting of leaves and stems, especially at the base of the plant, indicates that the plants have been consistently overwatered.

Immediately you see a yellowing, mottled, mouldy or mildewed leaf, or rotting stems or foliage, cut out the affected parts.

If you see any of the signs of pest damage indicated below, then examine the plant carefully. Turn the leaves over, as many pests feed on the underside of the leaves. If there are young tender leaves, say at the end of a shoot, look carefully among these for aphis (greenfly) and other pests. Naturally they tend to congregate and feed on tender young tissue.

As part of the general care of pot plants, clean the foliage regularly to remove dust. This can be a killer if plants are left too long with a layer of dust preventing the leaves from breathing. Wipe large leaves with a damp cloth. Plants with large numbers of small leaves may be stood out in the rain on warm days, or, holding your fingers firmly over the top of the pot to prevent the plant from falling out, draw the foliage to and fro several times in a sink filled with tepid water.

There are plenty of effective insecticides on the market – derris is a very safe control for aphis and most of the other pests likely to infest house plants. One of the easiest and most effective ways of destroying pests is by means of an aerosol spray. These are rather expensive but so little is used that the convenience outweighs the cost. With an aerosol the fine misty liquid penetrates between young leaves and under the foliage. Some insecticides, particularly any containing derris, are poisonous to fish, so if you have a fish bowl keep it covered when spraying your plants.

Symptoms of Trouble

Leaves turning yellow – dropping off.
>   Faulty watering – usually overwatering. Unsuitable temperature –
>   too cold in winter, wide fluctuations or draughty conditions.

Leaves yellowing or becoming streaked, spotted or mottled, brown at the edges.
>   Mechanical damage (breaks, cuts and abrasions), draughts.

Leaves covered with white or grey mould.
>   Mildew or *Botrytis* mould.

Leaves drooping or dropping off.
>   Drought, usually in summer; overwatering, usually in winter.

Leaves or stems rotting.
>   Usually caused by overwatering, sometimes as a result of
>   physical injury.

Flowers and buds dropping off.
>   Overwatering, too dry an atmosphere.

Leaves or buds eaten at edges, distorted.
>   Caused by pests – aphis (greenfly), white fly, thrips, mealy bugs, or
>   vine weevils.

Leaves tunnelled.
>   Leaf miner.

Leaves pale, brittle and minutely spotted.
>   Red spider or spider mite; worst in too dry conditions.

Plant pale, weak and spindly.
>   Lack of plant food. Too high temperatures. Too little light.

Sinningia, (Gloxinia), special hybrids

27

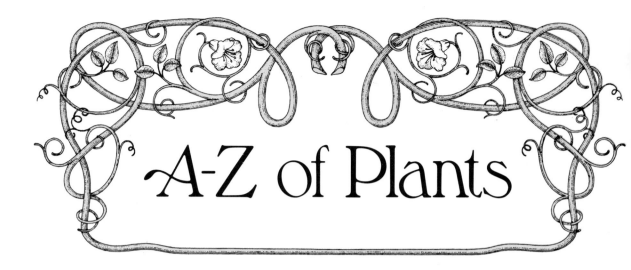

A-Z of Plants

Foliage House Plants

Aphelandra squarrosa
Distinctive pointed, white-veined leaves; flowers like bright yellow pineapples composed of overlapping bracts. Best in warm room in bright but not direct sunlight. Keep away from draughts.
Water freely in summer, feeding weekly until flowers form. Water sparingly in winter and hardly at all for about 10 weeks after the flowers fade. Raise new plants from shoot tip cuttings in gritty potting mixture in gentle heat.

Araucaria excelsa (Norfolk Island pine)
Christmas tree shape with slightly pendent branches clad with needle-like leaves. Thrives in full sun or semi-shade in normal room temperature. Water freely in spring and summer, less so when growth slows down in autumn and winter. Feed fortnightly in growing season with liquid fertilizer if growth poor.
Prevent it from becoming pot-bound and suffering, by repotting each spring, in a size larger pot. Raise new plants from seed.

Asparagus
Two kinds generally grown: *A. plumosus* with ferny fronds and *A. sprengeri* with leaves like pine needles. Grows well in sun or semi-shade; good for hanging baskets, draughty halls or ill-lit windowsills. Normal room temperature.
Keep soil moist throughout growing season or leaves inclined to yellow and fall. Let soil remain drier in winter. Feed weekly from spring to late summer.

Propagate from seeds sown in gentle heat or division of the rootstock.

Aspidistra (cast iron plant)
Broad, glossy spear-shaped leaves, green or striped creamy white. Does well in semi-shade and does not object to gas fumes. Will stay healthy even if neglected for many weeks. Normal room temperature. Freshen leaves by sponging them or spraying them occasionally with clear water.
Give ample water in spring and summer but less in winter.
Increase it by dividing the rootstock.

Begonia rex
Large heart-shaped leaves with irregular edges, patterned with cream, red or purple.
Develops most handsome foliage in moist, semi-shade conditions in normal room temperature.
Keep the soil moist in summer, but drier in winter. Feed fortnightly with dilute liquid fertilizer throughout the growing season.
Set pots inside larger ones, packing gaps with peat which is kept moist to encourage strong healthy growth. Dry air can cause leaves to wither and fall.
Propagate from leaf cuttings pegged flat on to sandy surface in gentle heat or cut into sections, each containing a main vein.

Bryophyllum
Spear-shaped leaves edged with baby plantlets. *B. daigremontianum* has leaves which are purplish red in colour and distinctly toothed. Pinkish yellow flowers borne in winter.
Set plants in good light at normal room temperature, watering frequently in summer, but less so in winter. No

feeding necessary.

Get new plants from the babies which are easily detached from the leaf margin, often complete with roots, and grow them on in small pots of potting mix.

Chlorophytum (spider plant)
Rosette of green, white-striped leaves. Pendent stems of creamy white flowers appear from the centre, often with plantlets at their tips. Established plants have a cascade of rosettes which look most effective from the top of a pedestal.

Tolerates light shade or bright hot conditions in which many other house plants would fail. Normal room temperature best.

Give plenty of water in summer, less in winter.

No feeding necessary if plant is set in good potting mix to start with. Root plantlets that form at ends of stems.

Cissus (kangaroo vine)
Two forms commonly grown: *C. antarctica* with shining spear-shaped leaves and *C. discolor* with triangular green leaves patterned silvery white and purple. Thrive in semi-shade or full sun.

Keep the soil moist during the growing season, but less so in autumn and winter. Feed once a fortnight if growth slow.

Normal room temperature.

Raise plants from stem cuttings.

Codiaeum (croton)
Broad or narrow glossy leaves variously patterned, flecked or striped with yellow or orange.

Needs evenly warm and moist atmosphere in good light. Bathroom or kitchen ideal. Keep the soil moist throughout the year and feed every ten days during the growing season. Sponge leaves to keep them bright and shining and spray them frequently with clear water in summer.

Good plan to set pot inside larger one, packing space with peat, keeping this moist. This lessens risk of leaf drop. Raise new plants from stem cuttings.

Coleus
Magnificent foliage plant. Leaves splashed or patterned red, green, yellow, purple, brown or black; heart-shaped with toothed or frilled edges. Grows well in good light position at normal room temperature.

Keep roots well watered in summer but drier in winter. Spray leaves with clear water during growing season but not in winter.

Propagate from stem cuttings or seeds sown in gentle heat.

Cyperus alternifolia (Madagascar umbrella plant)
Long thin stems topped by umbrella of leaves.

Set plants in good light in humid atmosphere. Keep out of full sun. Normal room temperature. Water freely in summer but keep soil drier in autumn and winter. Feed every 10–14 days throughout the growing season. Cut away fading leaves to make way for new growth.

Propagate from stem cuttings rooted in water, or by dividing the stock.

Dieffenbachia (dumb cane)
Large paddle-like leaves mottled green and white.

Light shade or good light, but not direct sunlight or leaves may shrivel. Normal room temperature, humid atmosphere.

Feed weekly throughout spring and summer and keep soil moist during the growing season, and in winter.

Raise new plants from suckers from base of plant or by rooting sections of the stem.

Dizygotheca elegantissima
Graceful long stemmed palmate leaves composed of narrow toothed 'fingers'. Green or reddish brown in colour.

Semi-shade in summer but have plants in good light in winter. Humid atmosphere necessary for strong growth, so ideally fit pots into larger ones, filling intervening space with peat which is kept moist.

Keep the soil moist in summer, dryish in winter. Normal room

temperature. Encourage handsome leaves by feeding every 10 days during the growing season.

Raise plants from stem cuttings.

Fatshedera lizei
Result of crossing an ivy (*Hedera*) with a *Fatsia*. Trailing habit. Leaves large, glossy, palmate.

Normal room temperature. Water freely throughout the year. Feed weekly and freshen leaves by sponging regularly. Keep plants shapely by nipping out growing point if they become too tall. Support growth with canes, wires or trellis-work.

Increase plants from stem cuttings.

Fatsia japonica (aralia, fig-leaved palm)
Dark green, shiny fingered leaves. Does well in semi-shade or good light. Normal room temperature. Water freely in spring and summer, less in autumn and winter.

Feed every 10 days and sponge leaves or spray them with clear water to keep them bright and fresh.

Increase from stem cuttings.

Ficus elastica (rubber plant)
Central stem set with broad, pointed leathery leaves that take a high gloss; there is a variegated form.

Best in good light but tolerates light shade. Normal room temperature. Water thoroughly, then leave until soil becomes dry on top. Keep soil fairly dry in winter.

Feed fortnightly from April to September. Either sponge leaves with water to keep them glossy and bright, or use proprietary leaf-cleaning substance.

Air layer top of plant if lower stem loses its leaves. Alternatively, raise new plants from stem or leaf cuttings.

Ficus pumila (creeping fig)
Creeping rubber plant with tiny heart-shaped leaves.

Grows well in light shade or full sun, in warm or cold room.

Give ample water in summer, less in winter. Feed weekly only if growth slow. Spray leaves with clear water if the air is hot and dry to prevent leaves curling.

Grow new plants from stem cuttings.

Gynura sarmentosa
Spreading plant with long nettle-like leaves with a silky purple sheen.

Grows well in baking sun; ideal for conservatories or sun lounges where few other plants can stand the dry heat. Normal room temperature. Water freely in summer, less in winter. Feed fortnightly from March to September.

Raise new plants from shoot tip cuttings.

Hedera helix (English ivy)
Glossy, green or variegated lobed and pointed leaves. Trailing plant for semi-shade, or good but not bright conditions. Looks well in hanging basket. Can be grown outdoors throughout the year. Spray leaves with clear water once a week if plants grown in warm dry room. This will prevent leaf drop and red spider attacks. Water freely in summer, less in winter. Feed weekly throughout the growing season.

Remove any green leaves which sprout up in variegated foliage varieties. Increase plants from stem cuttings. 'Glacier', 'Gloire de Marengo' and 'Chicago' are 3 of the brightest varieties.

Howea belmoreana (Kentia)
Graceful palm for warm conservatories or greenhouses. Fronds consist of central midribs set with numerous long and narrow leaflets about 12 to 15 inches (30–38 cm.) in length. Height of plant 10 feet (3 m.).

Frond stems around 18 inches (45 cm.) long.

Sun or shade, good rich soil to encourage luxuriant growth. Spray leaves frequently with warm water in spring and summer. Feed fortnightly with dilute liquid fertilizer. Normal room temperature.

Prune away dead leaves as they fade. Raise new plants from seeds.

Monstera deliciosa (Swiss cheese plant, hurricane plant)
Handsome climber with large sliced or perforated leaves. Occasionally a pine cone-like flower appears followed by a fruit which is edible and has a pineapple flavour. Prefers semi-shade in warm moist conditions at around normal room temperature. Keep the soil moist in summer and drier in winter.

Sponge the leaves frequently to keep them shining bright. Provide some form of support for the trailing stems which often grow attractive white aerial roots. Feed weekly throughout the growing season.

Raise new plants from cuttings.

Peperomia
Low growing plant with deep green crinkled and ribbed, heart-shaped leaves; creamy white-striped or mottled creamy yellowish leaves. White rat's tail flower spikes. *P. caperata*, *P. sandersii* and *P.*

magnoliaefolia most commonly grown for their striking foliage.

All do well in normal room temperature in good light or semi-shade. Water freely in summer, less in winter. Feed fortnightly if growth poor. Syringe leaves to freshen them and keep them free from dust.

Raise new plants from division of the parent plant or from cuttings.

Philodendron
Leaves glossy and of various shapes, as: *P. bipinnatifidum*, deeply fingered; *P. scandens*, heart-shaped; *P. melanochrysum*, large and narrowly shield-shaped. All thrive in good but not bright light or semi-shade, in a humid atmosphere at normal room temperature.

Give plenty of water in summer, but let soil dry so that it is just moist in winter. Feed weekly throughout spring and summer. Sponge and syringe the leaves frequently to enhance their appearance and keep down red spider mite. Provide support for the climbing stems.

Increase from stem and leaf cuttings.

Pilea cadierei
Oval leaves patterned with silver. Spreading plant for sunny windowsill; tolerates light shade.

Grows well in dry air conditions at normal room temperature. Water freely in spring and summer, slightly less in autumn and winter. Feed weekly during growing season. Increase from shoot tip cuttings.

Rhoicissus rhomboidea
Climber with tripartite diamond-shaped leaves. Good for hanging baskets, trailing from pedestals. Thrives in light shade or good but not direct light in normal room temperature. Give plenty of water in spring and summer, keeping soil just moist in winter. Feed fortnightly during the growing season if progress slow.

Raise new plants from stem cuttings.

Sansevieria (mother-in-law's tongue, snake plant)
Erect sword-shaped leaves. Three kinds usually grown: *S. trifasciata* has greyish white banded leaves, *S. trifasciata laurentii* has tall yellow-

Exacum affine

edged leaves, while *S. trifasciata hahnii* is much smaller with greenish grey banded leaves. Best at normal room temperature. Water very carefully at all times making sure not to over-wet the soil. Keep fairly dry in winter, just moist in summer.
Feed fortnightly throughout the spring and summer. Enjoys good light position though will tolerate semi-shade. Raise new plants from division or stem sections.

Scindapsus aureus
Climbing or trailing plant with fleshy, flecked and mottled creamy yellow variegated leaves.
Does well in good but not bright sunlight. Tends to lose its variegation in semi-shade. Normal room temperature.
Water freely in summer, less in winter. The soil should never be waterlogged. Encourage strong growth by feeding weekly throughout the spring and summer. Pinch out shoot tips of straggly shoots to encourage them to bush out.
Increase plants from stem cuttings.

Tradescantia (wandering Jew)
Two widely grown are *T. fluminensis*, with silver and green-striped leaves and *T. blossfeldiana*, with boat-shaped leaves dark purple beneath. Normal room temperature. Best in good but not bright sunlight. In semi-shade, leaves lose their colouring and remain pale grass-green.

Water to keep soil moist in summer but dryish in winter when growth slows down. Finest leaves in warm humid atmosphere of bathroom or steamy kitchen. Raise new plants from cuttings of shoot tips. Feed fortnightly throughout the growing season, from April to September.

Vriesea splendens (flaming sword)
Rosette of thick, narrow, dark green banded leaves from centre of which appears an ear-of-corn-like flower in red and yellow. Prefers semi-shade but tolerates bright but not direct sunlight. Normal room temperature. Water well in spring and summer, less so during winter. Fill funnel-shaped centre of leaf rosette with water to help flower spike form. After flower fades, the plant dies, to be followed by sucker growths around the edge. Detach these with roots and plant them out singly in small pots of peaty potting mix. Feed fortnightly while growing strongly and flowering.

Zebrina (wandering Jew)
Effective trailer with mauve, green and silver striped leaves, the undersides of which are shining purple.
Best in semi-shade or good light – not direct sunlight. Normal room temperature.
Water freely while plants growing strongly in spring and summer. Keep soil just moist in autumn and winter. Feed fortnightly throughout the growing season.

Raise new plants from shoot tip cuttings which strike easily.

Ferns

Adiantum (maidenhair fern)
Asplenium (bird's nest fern)
Nephrolepis (ladder fern)
Pteris (ribbon fern)
The above need similar treatment and thrive in light shade; they object to hot sunny conditions. Normal room temperature.
Water freely in both summer and winter, feeding weekly in spring and summer. Syringe fronds with water to keep them fresh in dry air.
Raise plants by dividing the rootstock; sowing spores.
Asplenium needs very warm moist conditions and thrives if set in larger pots packed with sphagnum moss which is kept watered.

Flowering House Plants

Azalea see Rhododendron

Begonia semperflorens
Splendid as a summer bedding plant or house plant for semi-shade or full sun. Red, white, or pink flowers massed on short stems clad with bright glossy green or bronzy foliage. Normal room temperature. Give plenty of water in summer, just

keeping soil moist in winter.
Feed every 7 days in summer and early autumn. Remove faded flowers to help others form.
Raise new plants from stem cuttings or division of the rootstock.

Beloperone guttata (shrimp plant)
Small arching stems with 'shrimp' or 'prawn' shaped flowers of brownish red overlapping bracts. In flower for many weeks at a time.
Needs position in full sun or shoots become leggy and flowerless. Normal room temperature, humid atmosphere. Water freely in spring and summer, less in winter. Feed weekly throughout the growing season. Shorten straggly shoots after flowering.
Raise new plants from cuttings.

Billbergia nutans (angel's tears, queen's tears)
Rosette of thin strap-shaped leaves and hanging carmine flowers with yellow centres.
Best in semi-shade or good but not direct sunlight. Water freely throughout the summer, less so in winter. Normal room temperature; able to withstand dry air of central heating. Feed fortnightly from April to September. After flowering the plant dies, but sucker shoots from the base can be planted out singly in small pots of gritty potting mix.

Campanula isophylla (star of Bethlehem)
Perfect for hanging baskets in light airy conditions. Starry blue or white bellflowers form freely on trailing stems. Normal room temperature; may be set outdoors in summer. Water freely in summer, but less so from late August onwards until fresh shoots appear. Feed fortnightly from mid-summer until fresh growth forms. Cut back fading flowers to encourage new shoots. Keep soil dryish and plant cool during resting period from early autumn to mid-winter. Increase plants from stem cuttings.

Capsicum (pepper)
Glossy red or yellow cone-shaped peppers; highly decorative. Best in bright sunshine at normal room temperature. Water freely in summer, spraying the leaves with clear water from time to time. Feed fortnightly throughout the spring and up until flowers form.

Raise new plants from seed each year. Old plants discarded after flowering.

Citrus mitis (Calamondin orange)
Scented white flowers followed by small golf ball-sized oranges. Leaves narrow, pointed, quite striking. Fruits form early in the life of this plant. Grows well in pots.
Living-room conditions in good light but not direct sun. Water freely in summer, syringing leaves occasionally, but keeping soil drier in winter. Feed fortnightly to encourage lustrous leaves.
Raise new plants from seed or cuttings.

Clivia (Kaffir lily)
Rosy red flowers born in umbels on top of stout fleshy stems. Strap-like leaves.
Best in good light in airy conditions at normal room temperature. Give ample water in summer, less in winter. Avoid saturating potting mixture. Encourage growth by feeding fortnightly throughout the spring and summer. Let soil become fairly dry and set plant in coolish spot from September to late December. Return to warmer conditions in spring and replace top inch of pot soil with fresh potting mix.
Increase from suckers at base of plant, or division of the rootstock.

Cyclamen persicum
Frilled or smooth pink, red purple or white flowers. Blooms borne on tubular fleshy stems from among handsome patterned and marbled leaves. Best in good light in airy conditions. Temperature critical: 13–16°C. (55–60°F.) ideal. If too hot and dry leaves rapidly yellow and wither.

Plunge pot rim deep outdoors in sunny position for the summer. No special watering needed throughout the summer. Bring indoors in August and repot in rich potting mixture. Water carefully in autumn and winter, making sure that the corm does not get too wet. Feed fortnightly throughout the autumn and winter period.
Raise new plants from seed.

Exacum affine
Small yellow-centred, blue-flowered plant with bright green leaves. Prefers semi-shade. Thrives at normal room temperature.
Give plenty of water in summer and feed fortnightly throughout the growing season.
This is grown as an annual and plants are raised from seed or cuttings.

Fuchsia
Fat or slender bell-shaped flowers like ballet skirts. Colours range from deep purple through scarlet, rosy red, pink, orange and white; there are even some with bluish tints.
Grows best in good light in airy conditions but will tolerate semi-shade. Water freely throughout the summer but keep soil dryish in winter when plants resting. Feed fortnightly during the spring and summer.
Prune back shoots in late winter, early spring and repot in fresh soil, watering well to encourage new growth.
Raise new plants from stem cuttings.

Geranium see **Pelargonium**

Gloxinia see **Sinningia**

Hippeastrum (amaryllis)
Flared trumpet-shaped flowers in vivid colours; sword-like leaves. Does well in good light position at normal room temperature.
Keep soil moist in spring and summer, but drier from August onwards until the leaves die back and the bulb rests until December.
When planting, set the bulb only halfway in the soil. Feed fortnightly from late winter to early autumn. The flowers are produced after Christmas and specially prepared bulbs will flower a few weeks earlier than unprepared bulbs.

Hoya carnosa (Japanese wax or honey flower)

Climbing evergreen whose broad leathery leaves offset rounded clusters of starry, pale pink flowers. Rich fragrance. Light, sunny position best; ideal for hanging baskets. Normal room temperature in summer, cooler in winter. Water freely throughout the growing season but less so in winter. Feed every 10 days with dilute liquid fertilizer, from late winter to September. Train stems round a wire support up canes.
Raise new plants from stem cuttings.

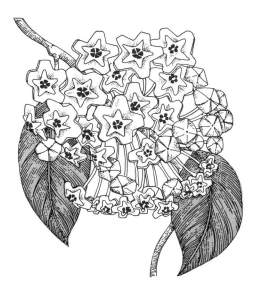

Hydrangea hortensis (H. macrophylla)
The florist's hydrangea has very large, usually single or occasionally double ball-headed blooms on short stems around 9 inches (23 cm.) high. Colours: shades of blue, red, pink and white. Give it a cool light airy position when in flower and feed weekly with dilute liquid fertilizer to prolong the display. Blooms appear over the winter period. Change pink varieties to a deep, ultramarine-blue by adding a teaspoonful of alum to the pot soil and watering this in.
After flowering, shorten the shoots to leave one or two pairs of leaves above the older wood. Continue to feed and water to sustain new growth.
Set the plant outdoors in a lightly shaded spot for the summer and bring indoors in September for plant to flower again.
Raise new plants from stem cuttings in early summer.

Impatiens sultanii (busy lizzie)
Popular flowering house plant that almost thrives on neglect. Fleshy stems set with myriads of pinkish rose, scarlet, carmine, orange or violet flowers.

Set in full sun to encourage free flowering. Normal room temperature, humid atmosphere. Pinch out growing tips to encourage branching. Feed weekly throughout the growing season from March to September. Water freely throughout the summer, less in winter or stems may rot. Increase from seeds or stem cuttings.

Pelargonium (geranium)
Geranium is the common misnomer for *Pelargonium*. There are three distinct kinds: ivy-leaved; zonal, with banded leaves; and regal, with more irregularly shaped leaves. The latter is tender and is best grown indoors in light airy conditions at normal room temperature. Both the zonal and ivy-leaved may be grown indoors or bedded out for the summer.
Their flowers are brilliantly hued, orange, pink, white and red. All do well in good light.
Water freely in summer, drying off plants for the winter, unless they are rooted cuttings when they should be kept just moist.
Feed weekly throughout the growing season.
Dig up plants in early autumn when nights grow cool and overwinter them in boxes of soil in a frost-free greenhouse or cold, not freezing, well-lit room.
Take cuttings in August.

Primula obconica
Clusters of rose-pink, red, blue or white flowers in bloom throughout the year. Leaves rounded and slightly hairy. Most reliable house plant. Give it a position in full light at normal room temperature. Water freely in summer, less so in winter. Feed every 7 days in summer.
This primula can cause the skin to develop a rash. Do not grow it if you are allergic to it. Cut back the faded flowers, and pot on in spring if roots are filling the pot. Raise new plants from seed.

Rhododendron indicum
This is the correct name for the plant still probably better known as *Azalea indica*.
Single or double peony-like flowers massed on short stems. Evergreen shrub. Does best in good light or semi-shade. Normal room temperature, humid atmosphere. Spray leaves if the air is hot and dry.

Feed fortnightly while flowers are forming and water freely. After flowering, put plant in unheated but frost-free place, watering less and withholding feed. The soil must not become too dry. Remove dead flowers. Sink pot outdoors in the soil for the summer and continue to feed and water regularly. Bring it back inside in September and repot in peaty soil. Give ample water and feed fortnightly while new growth is forming and flower buds developing.

Saintpaulia (African violet)
Single or double flowers in many shades including pink, carmine, scarlet, cream and azure-blue. Leaves hairy, greyish green.
Thrives in semi-shade or good but not bright sunlight. Flourishes in a humid atmosphere and benefits from an occasional steam bath.
Water whenever the soil is dry in summer, but sparingly in autumn and winter, especially after flowering. Avoid splashing the leaves with water as this can cause brown patches to develop. Summer temperature 18–21°C. (65–70°F.); reduce to 13°C. (55°F.) in autumn and winter.
Feed fortnightly throughout the spring and early summer.
Increase from leaf cuttings.

Saxifraga stolonifera (syn. *S. sarmentosa*) (mother-of-thousands)
Round reddish green, white veined leaves that form an almost flat rosette, from the centre of which slender upright stems of white butterfly-like flower sprays appear.
Ideal for hanging baskets in good but not full sun. Normal room temperature. Keep the soil moist in summer and dryish in winter. Feed fortnightly throughout the spring and summer.
Cut away fading leaves to allow fresh ones to replace them. Young leaves also have brighter markings.
Set out plantlets that form on wiry stems from the centre of the plant.

Sinningia (gloxinia)
Red, blue, white or pink, bell-shaped flowers with plain or frilled petals edged white in some varieties.
Best in light shade away from direct sun, or leaves will flop. Humid atmosphere desirable. Normal room temperature.
Water to keep soil moist in spring and

summer, feeding fortnightly to encourage long flowering and strong healthy growth. In autumn when the flowers fade and leaves wither and die back, cease watering and keep the soil quite dry over winter.

In March, start tubers into growth once more in a tray of moist peat in a warm, moist place. When they are sprouting freely, repot the tubers in peaty potting mix. Pinch out all but the three strongest shoots which are left to form a sturdy plant.

Raise new plants from leaf cuttings or seeds.

Solanum (Christmas cherry)
Popular pot plant for Christmas with orange-red marble-sized berries set on shoot tips amid dark green leaves. Best in bright airy position at normal room temperature. Water freely whenever the soil is dry and spray the flowers to encourage a good set of fruits. Feed every 10 days when flower buds are forming.

Cut back fruited shoots to an inch or two of the main framework, when the berries are over.

Raise from seed or cuttings.

Streptocarpus (Cape primrose)
Striking blue, pink, white or violet trumpet flowers, some attractively veined, on long slender stems. Crinkly primrose-like leaves. Place in semi-shade in humid atmosphere at normal room temperature. Water liberally in summer, hardly at all in winter, or just sufficient to prevent soil getting too dry.

Feed fortnightly when flower buds forming. Rest plant from October to March, in cool, dryish conditions.

Raise new plants from seeds or leaf cuttings.

Thunbergia alata (black-eyed Susan)
Open orange-yellow black-centred flowers borne freely on trailing stems. Best in light airy position. Looks well in hanging baskets or cascading from window boxes. Normal room temperature. Give plenty of water throughout the growing season and feed fortnightly to encourage strong growth and many flowers.

Raise from seeds each spring and pot on singly in small pots. Nip out growing tip to make plant branch and form several flowering shoots.

Discard after flowering.

Cacti

Epiphyllum
Cactus hybrids with yellow, white, pink and crimson-hued flowers like flamboyant waterlilies. Fleshy jointed stems, flattened and waved at the edges. Best in diffused light; will tolerate light shade. Normal room temperature. Water freely throughout the growing season, and keep the soil fairly moist in winter. Feed weekly from April to September.

Repot annually when flowers fade. Raise new plants from seeds or cuttings.

Mammillaria
This cactus forms its flowers in a ring on top of the plant. They are bell-like with flared petals and mostly purplish, red or creamy white. Full sun and normal room temperature. Water freely in summer but hardly at all in winter.

No feeding necessary unless growth is slow. Raise new plants from cuttings.

Rebutia
Brilliant coloured trumpet flowers in all shades of pink, orange, red and yellow. Blooms last about a week and are freely produced. Cactus body globe-shaped, set with minute spines and hairs. Thrives in full sun, at normal room temperature. Ideal for hot dry conditions.

Water freely from April to September,

keeping the soil fairly dry for the rest of the year. Feed fortnightly if growth slow.

Raise new plants from cuttings.

Rhipsalidopsis (Easter cactus)
Scarlet trumpet flowers borne at the tips of thick, fleshy jointed leaves. Grows best in full sun but will tolerate light shade. Normal room temperature. Water freely throughout the spring and summer but less so during autumn and winter, particularly from December to January when shoots are ripening and flower buds forming.

Feed every ten days from late spring to autumn.

Propagate new plants from leaf cuttings snapped off at a joint.

Schlumbergera (*Zygocactus*, Christmas cactus, crab cactus)
Magenta-rose fuchsia-like flowers borne at the tips of pendent fleshy jointed stems.

Good but not direct sunlight, normal room temperature.

Water freely in spring, sparingly from June to August. Keep soil fairly dry in winter but water freely when flower buds appear. Spray foliage with clear water to keep plants fresh in hot dry air of centrally heated room.

Feed only if growth is slow and then during the late spring and summer. Increase plants from stem cuttings broken off at a joint.

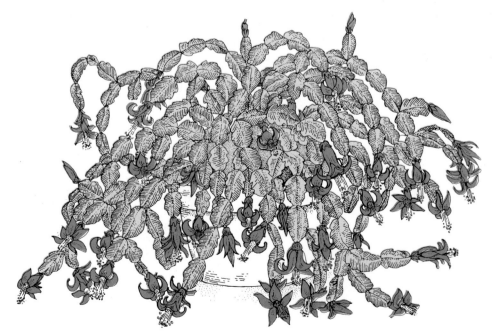

(right) Full advantage has been made here of plants with, in the foreground, the greyish *Ballota pseudodictamnus*

Container
Gardening
Outdoors

16

Using Containers

For many people living in the city, the possibilities of growing plants in containers placed wherever space is available outside can be a rewarding compensation for the lack of a garden or patio. Many plants, from small trees and flowering climbers to vegetables, fruit and herbs can be grown on roof gardens or balconies, in window boxes or hanging baskets, or in a tub outside the front door.

Hanging Baskets

These may often be accommodated in a porch or fixed to the wall outside a window.

It is possible to have a show of plants in a hanging basket in the spring if you are prepared to go and buy plants on the point of flowering – primroses, large-flowered daisies, forget-me-nots and, of course, a few bulbs if these have been planted in the basket in the autumn.

Hanging baskets are however usually used for summer-flowering plants. They can be made most attractive with a few upright plants combined with one or two trailers. Good plants which will bloom in a basket all through summer are fuchsias, begonias, particularly the varieties of *Begonia pendula*, ivy-leaved geraniums to hang down and one or two more upright geraniums, lobelias, both the dwarf and the trailing type and both the dwarf and trailing nasturtiums are excellent for hanging baskets.

For easy watering, the baskets may be suspended from the roof of a porch by a rope passed over a pulley which can be used to lower the basket.

Hanging baskets are made of galvanized or plastic-covered wire or of solid plastic material. Some of the latter have a kind of built-in saucer at the base which will catch any surplus water as it drains out of the 'basket' proper. The wire baskets may be lined with sphagnum moss before being filled with potting mix and this gives them a very attractive appearance. Alternatively

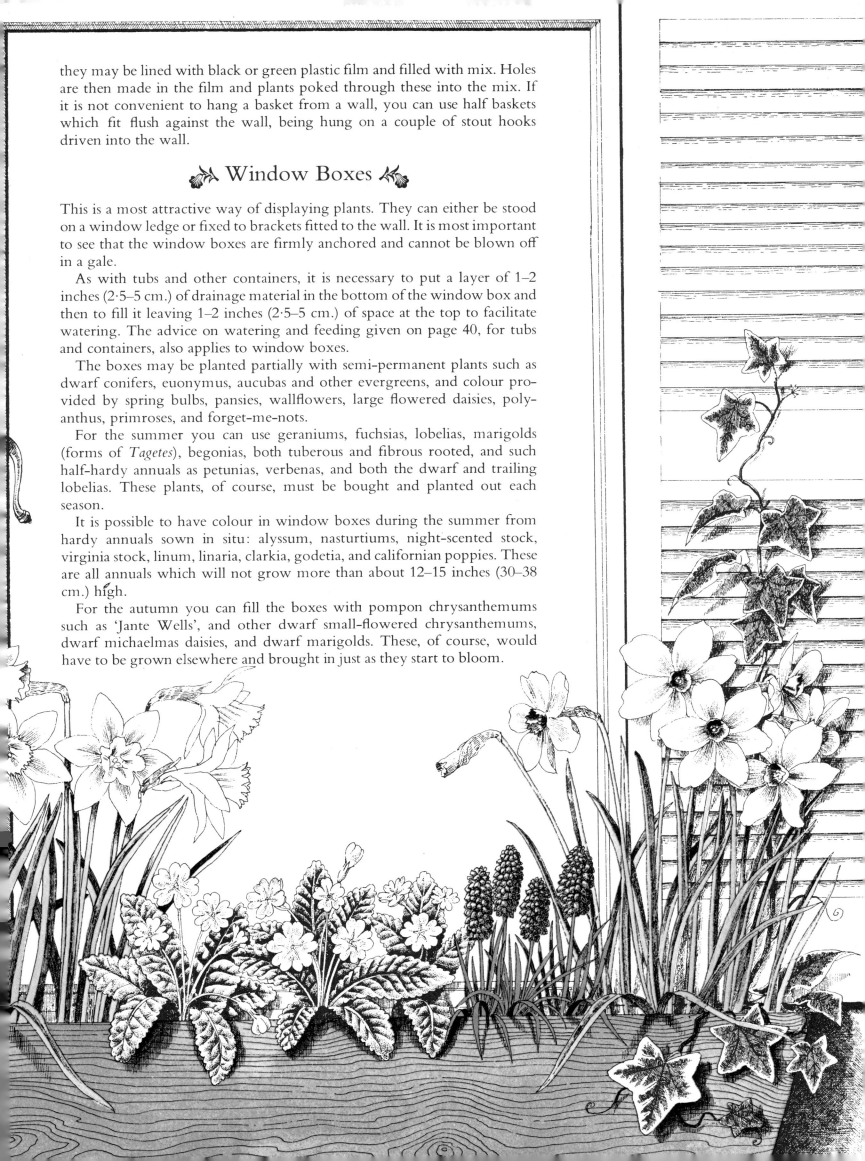

they may be lined with black or green plastic film and filled with mix. Holes are then made in the film and plants poked through these into the mix. If it is not convenient to hang a basket from a wall, you can use half baskets which fit flush against the wall, being hung on a couple of stout hooks driven into the wall.

Window Boxes

This is a most attractive way of displaying plants. They can either be stood on a window ledge or fixed to brackets fitted to the wall. It is most important to see that the window boxes are firmly anchored and cannot be blown off in a gale.

As with tubs and other containers, it is necessary to put a layer of 1–2 inches (2·5–5 cm.) of drainage material in the bottom of the window box and then to fill it leaving 1–2 inches (2·5–5 cm.) of space at the top to facilitate watering. The advice on watering and feeding given on page 40, for tubs and containers, also applies to window boxes.

The boxes may be planted partially with semi-permanent plants such as dwarf conifers, euonymus, aucubas and other evergreens, and colour provided by spring bulbs, pansies, wallflowers, large flowered daisies, polyanthus, primroses, and forget-me-nots.

For the summer you can use geraniums, fuchsias, lobelias, marigolds (forms of *Tagetes*), begonias, both tuberous and fibrous rooted, and such half-hardy annuals as petunias, verbenas, and both the dwarf and trailing lobelias. These plants, of course, must be bought and planted out each season.

It is possible to have colour in window boxes during the summer from hardy annuals sown in situ: alyssum, nasturtiums, night-scented stock, virginia stock, linum, linaria, clarkia, godetia, and californian poppies. These are all annuals which will not grow more than about 12–15 inches (30–38 cm.) high.

For the autumn you can fill the boxes with pompon chrysanthemums such as 'Jante Wells', and other dwarf small-flowered chrysanthemums, dwarf michaelmas daisies, and dwarf marigolds. These, of course, would have to be grown elsewhere and brought in just as they start to bloom.

(above) Fuchsias and begonias form the prominent colour feature of this container planting

(right) This wheel-barrow is planted with lobelia, petunia, fuchsia and ivy-leaved geraniums

(far right) Ivy has been trained up the outside wall of this house and petunias and geraniums planted in the tubs

Tubs and Containers

The various types available are perhaps the mainstay of the city gardener. Available in different sizes, shapes and materials, they are useful both where space is limited, as on the balcony, roof garden or in front of the house and also in a larger area, such as a back yard or patio where the garden soil may be very poor.

Naturally the types of plants to be grown depends largely on the size of the tub. A tub, say, up to 2½ feet (75 cm.) across and about 2 feet (60 cm.) deep can accommodate a wide range of shrubs, climbers or even a small tree. Smaller tubs will of course contain smaller shrubs as well as bulbs and bedding plants.

Tubs, like window boxes and other containers, are made from a wide variety of materials. Wood is popular but there are also troughs made of concrete and various plastic materials including glass-fibre moulded from antique lead containers. All containers should be checked for adequate drainage holes.

The self-watering plastic troughs are a splendid invention: you can fill the reservoir with water and it will supply the plants' needs for 2–3 weeks.

It is worth shopping around wine merchants, large hotels or restaurants as empty wine or beer casks may often be bought quite reasonably. These are then easily cut in half to make plant containers. Tie a piece of string round the middle of the barrel and draw a chalk line along it as a guide when sawing. Drainage holes, 1 inch (2·5 cm.) in diameter, should be bored in the bottom of the tubs, about 6 inches (15 cm.) apart. Treat the woodwork inside and out with a wood preservative – not creosote. Either leave the tubs their natural colour or paint the outside whatever colour you like. Treat the metal bands with a rust-proofing fluid before giving them a coat of paint. Place some pieces of broken flower pot or stones over the holes and then put in a layer of broken bricks, stones or similar material about 4–6 inches (10–15 cm.) deep. This is to ensure adequate drainage since otherwise the tub can become waterlogged after heavy rains.

On top of the drainage layer fill the tub to within about 2 inches (5 cm.) of the top with a proprietary potting mix. The peat-based composts are lighter than the loam-based mixes. If loam-based mixes are used it is wise to fill the tub rather less full, say to 3–4 inches (7·5–10 cm.) from the top and then place a layer of 1–2 inches (2·5–5 cm.) of peat on top of the mix. This

helps to keep it from drying out so quickly and thus reduces the need to water quite so often. Moisten the soil before applying a fertilizer – never put liquid fertilizer onto dry soil as this may damage the tender roots. Some people prefer to apply the fertilizer twice as often as the makers recommend but at half the recommended strength.

An attractive container can be made by the simple transformation of an old glazed sink into a good imitation of a stone one. Glazed sinks can often be acquired through a plumber since they are usually replaced when a kitchen is modernized. You should first wash and dry the sink thoroughly. Then mix together 2 parts of fine sphagnum peat, 1 part builders' sand, 1 part cement (all parts by weight) and add enough water to make the mixture thoroughly moist but not wet and sloppy. Coat the sink with a bonding material (from hardware stores) to make the surface sticky, then apply the peat mix, moulding it to the outer surface of the sink and down about 3–4 inches (7·5–10 cm.) inside. Just before the coating dries, if desired it can be scratched or marked with a brush or chisel to simulate old stone. A 9 litre bucketful of the peat mix should be enough for an ordinary domestic sink.

All the plants mentioned for growing in window boxes are suitable for growing in tubs. With the deeper soil one can, of course, grow shrubs of many kinds, as described on page 60, and also climbers.

Many people have a wish to grow a waterlily, or one or two other water plants, and it is possible to do so in a large tub. If you are using a wooden cask or barrel cut in half, the inside should be well charred before the tub is filled with water and planted.

The charring consists of lighting a fire of paper and kindling wood inside the tub, and letting it burn until the wood is charred to a depth of about $\frac{1}{8}$ inch (3 mm.).

Several small or miniature waterlilies are suitable for growing in a tub in a water depth of about 18 inches (45 cm.). The pink *Nymphaea x laydekeri* 'Lilacea', *N. x l.* 'Fulgens', a red variety, the sweetly scented *N. odorata* 'Minor' with white flowers, and the really miniature *N. pygmaea* 'Alba', white, and *N.p.* 'Helvola', primrose yellow, are all suitable for a tub, but only one plant would be needed for a tub, say, 2–2½ feet (60–75 cm.) across.

The waterlilies should be planted in a plastic pot in a loam-based mix.

It is desirable also to have in the tub 1–2 oxygenating plants, such as the water hawthorn, *Aponogeton distachyus*. You can also have, of course, a few fish – goldfish, shubunkins or golden orfe.

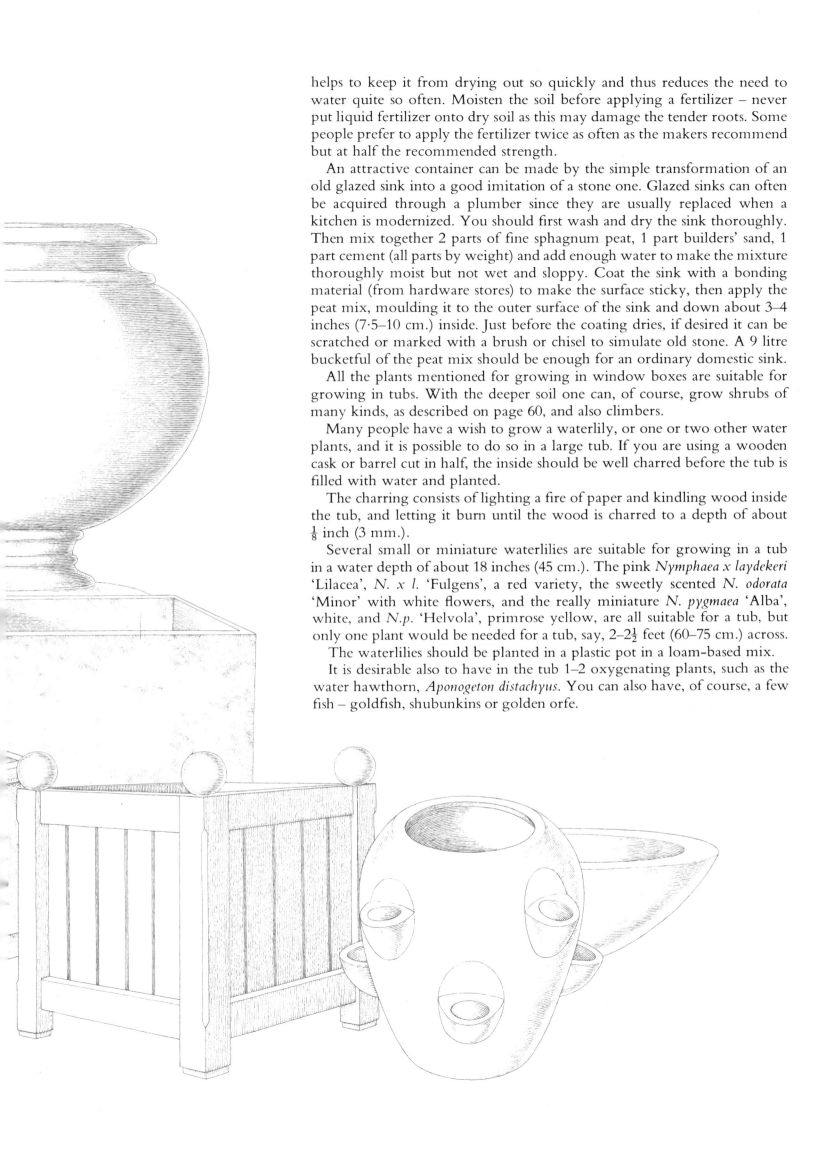

(left) This tiny area has been made an oasis of colour and luxurious foliage with clever and varied planting. All kinds of plants have been used – from a standard rose to a dwarf conifer – and every advantage has been made of the available space

(below) *Cistus*

❧ Roof Gardens ❧

Another possibility for the city gardener, this one poses its own initial problem. Unless it has been envisaged that the roof of say the house or garage would be used as a roof garden and the structure built to take the weight of containers and people, the roof may not be strong enough. It may of course be possible to reinforce it but this could be expensive. In any case unless you know that the roof is strong enough to support a roof garden, have an architect or builder inspect it before you try to grow anything on it.

Given a solid enough structure, however, it is amazing what can be grown on a roof garden in tubs and other containers. Where there is room you can even have grass, a small pool with fish, a fountain and flood lighting. Trees may be grown with success, up to 10 feet (3 m.) or so in height and a wide range of flowers, vegetables and even some fruits may be grown.

❧ Balconies ❧

These may be used and decorated in a number of ways by the city gardener. Plant pot-holders are available which may be attached to the railings or walls of the balcony. It is also possible to attach a square mesh panel of plastic-covered wire to the wall, fixing it to hooks so that it is an inch (about 2·5 cm.) or so away from the wall. Rings of plastic-covered wire may then be clipped on to the mesh and pot plants placed in the rings which are pliable and thus able to hold pots of various diameters. Quite a large number of pots can, in this way, be suspended in a small area.

If the balcony is capable of sustaining the weight of a number of pots, tubs and window boxes, it is possible to make a brave show by growing plants to flower in summer, and also having evergreens to look out upon

during the winter. You may, for example, in a large pot or tub, have a climbing plant such as an ivy or a virginia creeper to grow up the wall on either side of the balcony.

All the plants mentioned for growing in tubs and window boxes may be grown on a balcony, or indeed in a roof garden.

Miniature Rock Gardens

When made in a stone sink container these can give much pleasure. It should be filled with a good potting mixture, small pieces of rock placed here and there and the surface of the soil 'landscaped' to make shallow valleys and slight promontories.

There are rock plants that grow well in a stone sink, such as *Aethionema* 'Warley Rose', *Androsace lanuginosa*, *Campanula arvatica* and *C. pulla*, *Erinus alpinus*, *Silene acaulis*.

If you wish to include a miniature tree, the dwarf willow, *Salix x boydii* is suitable. The dwarf conifers are also excellent for sink gardens – *Chamaecyparis obtusa* and its varieties, *C. pisifera* 'Nana', *C. p.* 'Plumosa Compressa', *Juniperus communis*, 'Compressa'.

You can also grow many of the small bulbs, such as *Narcissus minimus*, crocuses, snowdrops, *Iris reticulata* and *I. histrioides*. Miniature roses will also do very well and the various saxifrages, armerias and the dwarf geraniums, such as *G. napuligerum*, will grow very happily in a miniature rock garden.

If the sink is filled with an acid soil you can grow the acid-loving plants which cannot be grown in an ordinary potting mix. A number of plants will happily tolerate an acid soil but most of the gentians, some of the dwarf rhododendrons, the acid-loving heathers, forms of *Erica*, *Calluna* and *Daboecia* must have an acid soil.

Plants for Containers

🌾 Permanent Plants 🌾

A surprisingly large number of permanent plants may be grown in containers, provided these are large and deep enough. Suggestions about the size of tubs and their treatment are given on pages 40–41.

The advantage of growing plants in containers in city gardens – or in gardens anywhere for that matter – is that you can grow plants that require a certain type of soil in separate containers. For example, rhododendrons, azaleas, camellias, gentians and heathers, all of which grow well in tubs in the city, provided the air is not too polluted, need an acid soil. This is provided by mixing plenty of peat moss with ordinary garden soil. When feeding is necessary an application of an acid fertilizer such as sulphate of ammonia should be given.

Practically no plants which the amateur is likely to wish to grow in the city insist on a purely alkaline soil. While there are many that will tolerate an alkaline soil, they will also grow quite well in the ordinary fertile soil of the garden. It is unusual to find soils in cities so alkaline as to prove unacceptable to all but plants that insist on a truly acid soil. As a rule, years of atmospheric pollution have resulted in the precipitation by means of the rainfall of the sulphuric acid which is polluting the atmosphere, and has made the city soil very often unacceptably acid for many garden plants. Usually, for this and other reasons, it is desirable for tubs and other containers to import good soil – one of the potting mixtures is ideal.

Another point in favour of using permanent shrubs in containers is that it is possible, if there is room to spare, to have some evergreen shrubs growing in an inconspicuous corner and have them brought into a more prominent position for the winter months when the last of the summer flowers are over and the spring flowers have not yet begun.

It is not, of course, necessary to have a number of pots for this purpose. It is quite possible to plant the shrubs such as dwarf conifers in any old container – a tin box with holes in the bottom for instance, or cheap plastic containers – which may be slipped inside the more ornamental tub or trough.

Many consumer goods, such as radios and other pieces of household equipment, now come packed in moulded polystyrene containers within a cardboard outer pack. These polystyrene packs are excellent for growing plants in, provided of course that they are deep enough and that holes can be bored through the bottom for drainage. It is important to note however that these containers burn very easily, so they should not be used indoors.

It is both easy and very effective to grow a few permanent plants in a tub or other container, provided there is room, and then plant flowers for spring, to be replaced by flowers for summer and autumn, around the permanent occupants. The dwarf conifers, variegated *Euonymus*, the golden *Lonicera* are excellent for this purpose.

Other charming permanent occupants of containers are the trailing plants which are evergreen and add another dimension to the display. The ivies are the most popular for this purpose, and it is better to use the smaller leaved varieties, unless of course the container is very large or unless the ivies are required to grow up a wall or other vertical support. The variegated

Snowdrops and winter aconite in container

ivies are most attractive and can be mixed judiciously with the green form. The variety 'Gold Heart' ('Jubilee') is particularly attractive and contrasts well with the small silvery-grey white-edged variety 'Glacier'. Other trailing plants that may be grown in tubs include the Creeping Jenny, *Lysimachia nummularia*, which has attractive yellow flowers in summer. There is also a golden variegated form.

Provided the containers are of a reasonable size and filled with a suitable potting mix, and the plants are fed regularly, it is possible to grow quite a range of wall shrubs and climbers for covering walls or trellises. These include of course the ivies already mentioned, as well as, here, the variety 'Gloire de Marengo' also known as *Hedera canariensis* 'Variegata', and there are also the Virginia creepers and the climbing hydrangea, *Hydrangea petiolaris*. All these climbers attach themselves to the walls or other supports

47

by means of aerial roots. They are not particularly good at clinging to shiny surfaces such as plastic covered wire or similar materials.

Where for example square-meshed plastic covered panels are used for supporting climbers, it is better to use the twining plants such as honeysuckle or clematis which attach themselves to their supports by twisting themselves or their leaf stem around the wire or whatever support is available.

❧ Plants for Spring Flowering ❧

It is the plants for spring flowering, which have to pass the winter in their containers, that are most harshly treated by the weather and which suffer most from impurities in the atmosphere. In cities with a heavily polluted atmosphere the old golden rule of growing plants which go underground in the winter is still very sound. Here of course the bulbs come into their own. Much depends upon the size of the containers whether one can grow permanent herbaceous plants which can be cut down every autumn and which pass the winter safely underground. The majority of these plants flower in summer or early autumn, and it is usually better to stick to bulbs and biennials for the spring display. There are, however, some perennial plants such as aubrieta, bergenia, arabis, and the yellow *Alyssum saxatile*, which are charming in the spring.

If the atmosphere is fairly clean one can plant wallflowers, forget-me-nots, sweet williams, pansies and the large-flowered daisies in the autumn as well as many bulbs. If the atmosphere, however, is very dirty, it is probably best to order some of these plants for collection in the spring, and plant them say in March, or early April when they will soon be in flower.

It is particularly with the spring flowers that it is a good plan to have several 'liners', that is containers which can be placed inside the tub, window box, or other container. The spring flowers do not last very long. Snowdrops probably last the longest as they start to flower at the turn of the year and go on for 2 months. Crocuses, winter aconites (*Eranthis*), and *Anemone blanda* are also flowers of the early spring and succeed well in containers. But as the weather warms up, the daffodils and tulips do not last so long, especially if one runs into a sunny period. For this reason it is a good idea to have a number of spare boxes which can be filled with a succession of daffodils and tulips.

❧ Plants for Summer Flowering ❧

For our purpose let us define summer as beginning at the end of May or early June, and ending when the frosts come, maybe any time from the end of September until early November, depending upon the season and where you live.

The spring flowers, the tulips, wallflowers and the forget-me-nots will have been past their best by the end of May or in colder districts some time in the first week of June. When they are removed you can take the opportunity of adding an organic fertilizer of some kind to the soil, as it is better to do this in the spring in readiness for filling the boxes again in the autumn. The reason is that the plant food will get the summer flowers away to a good start, and there should be enough left in the soil for the spring flowers which are planted in the autumn. It is not wise to plant flowers for spring in too rich a soil as this would encourage them to make soft growth that would be liable to damage in the winter from drying cold winds and frost.

As with all containers it is desirable to have some plants growing up and some hanging down. The most popular plants for bedding in tubs or boxes, or indeed in hanging baskets, are geraniums, fuchsias, lobelias – the tufted

48

and the trailing type, ageratums, petunias, and begonias. All the summer flowers thrive in the sun, although some of them will give quite a good account of themselves in shade or in semi-shade, in positions where the sun reaches them during some part of the day.

There are several ways of going about planting containers with summer flowers.

You can buy geraniums, petunias, begonias, fuchsias and the like and plant these after the spring flowers are over when dangers of frost are past. Some of these flowers, notably geraniums, fuchsias and begonias may be lifted and kept throughout the winter indoors, to be planted out again the following year. If plants are to be bought each year then there is much to be said for a combination of permanent occupants – say dwarf conifers in small window boxes or troughs, larger shrubs such as hydrangeas, or a box bush in the larger containers. Then fewer flowering plants are required to fill the container and while the result may not be so colourful and bright, the foliage plants do set off the brilliant colours of the flowers to advantage.

The cheapest way of filling a window box for summer effect is to use hardy annuals sown in situ. Here again the advantage of having a 'liner' is obvious. Most of the hardy annuals would be sown in March, and some of the half-hardy ones in April or, in cold districts, in May. Obviously if the containers are filled with spring flowers it is not possible to do this unless you have interchangeable 'liners'. But if the expense is a problem and you do not wish to buy considerable numbers of bedding plants, much pleasure can be obtained from hardy and half-hardy annuals sown in troughs or tubs.

Even if only 1 or 2 containers are available, it is worthwhile sowing the seeds of the scented annuals – alyssum, white or purple; mignonette, delightfully scented although a drab looking plant, and night-scented stock. One of the drawbacks about the flowers from seed is that many of them although very attractive do not last very long in bloom. Some, however, do carry on for many weeks, and some like alyssum, linaria and calendulas may be clipped over with a pair of scissors when the first flush of flowers is over, and more flowers will appear. Indeed it is possible to have 3 crops of bloom this way.

Some flowers like nasturtiums, both the dwarf bushy little plants and the trailing type, flower over a long period, as do the sweet peas – the Jet Set varieties – provided the dead flowers are assiduously picked off. The hardy annual chrysanthemums also flower over a long period, and godetias, clarkias, californian poppies and the morning glories or convolvulus last well, but again it is necessary to keep picking off the faded flowers.

For fairly large containers the miniature and Butterfly types of gladiolus are suitable. Unless the containers are in a very windy spot, if the corms are planted about 5 inches (12·5 cm.) deep they will need no support. These gladioli are of course a good investment as they may be lifted and kept through the winter for planting again the following year.

The dwarf bedding dahlias of the Coltness Gem type – there are both single and double dwarf forms – are excellent for providing colour from August until the coming of the frosts. They may be raised from seed if you have the facilities – see page 22 – or boxes of seedlings may be purchased. The plants may be lifted at the end of the season and the tubers stored in a frostproof place for planting out again the following year. They may be increased of course by cuttings taken in the spring.

To give colour well into the autumn, the dwarf marigolds or *Tagetes*, and the dwarf michaelmas daisies are excellent. The tagetes, being half-hardy annuals, will probably be planted out of boxes at the end of May or early June, but the michaelmas daisies, being hardy perennials, may form part of the permanent feature of the containers.

(far left) High up above the city this balcony, with a variety of containers and plants, affords privacy

(left) A gaily coloured window box includes fuchsia, lobelia and ivy-leaved geraniums

(below) This balcony, attractively filled with plants of varying heights, gives pleasure from outside and within the room

Fruits, Vegetables and Herbs

It is possible to grow some kind of fruits, vegetables and herbs quite satisfactorily in containers. There are others which people yearn to grow and which can, in fact, be grown but with mediocre results. However, working on the theory that half a lettuce is better than no lettuce many people are no doubt satisfied with some small result.

Fruit

Perhaps the first fruit a city dweller thinks of growing in a container is the strawberry. In days gone by people used to cut holes 1–2 inches (2·5–5 cm.) across in the side of a large barrel, fill it with soil and plant strawberry plants in the holes. Very pretty and productive they were too. But nowadays wooden casks are becoming scarcer and so are handymen who could cut the holes although it is possible to buy wooden strawberry barrels with holes. Various substitutes have appeared too, notably plastic containers which can be stacked one on top of the other making a tower of strawberry plants. Then from time to time containers of earthenware, concrete or reconstituted stone, with holes for the plants, have appeared on the market. Growing strawberries in containers really only makes sense if the container is of a vertical nature, so that a dozen or more plants can be grown on a very small area such as a balcony or roof.

Then a fig, 'Brown Turkey', will grow quite well, in milder areas, in a large tub. It may be cut down in a severe winter but would probably grow again, from the base.

A grape vine may also be grown in a tub, either trained against a wall or over an umbrella-shaped wire frame as you might grow weeping standard roses.

In all cases these fruits should be grown in full sun.

Apples, pears, peaches, apricots and plums may be grown in large pots or tubs. Naturally this calls for careful pruning and general care and a reliable nurseryman should be consulted about varieties to choose. He should be told that the trees are intended for pot culture and in the case of apples, should supply trees on dwarfing stocks, preferably 'Malling IX' for apples. Melons too may be grown in a tub, trough or similar sized container and for this the variety 'Ogen' or 'Charentais' would be the best to try.

Vegetables

Given containers of reasonable size – not less than a normal sized window box or a 9–10 inch (23–25 cm.) pot – and a reasonably sunny situation, many vegetables may be grown in a small area. Runner beans, however, may be grown in shade.

Probably the most rewarding are the salad vegetables. Tomatoes do very well in containers, usually ripening 4 trusses of fruit in warm areas. There are dwarf varieties, such as 'Pixie' which grows only to about 2 feet (60 cm.) in height or 'Tiny Tim' which grows to about 15 inches (38 cm.) and these are suitable for growing in a window box. The normal sized outdoor tomatoes are really only suitable for growing in troughs or tubs on a balcony or roof.

Lettuce grow well in containers and any of the smaller cabbage varieties are suitable. They need plenty of water and should not be allowed to dry out.

Capsicums, or sweet peppers, are excellent for growing in a large pot 8–9 inches (20–23 cm.) in diameter – or a reasonably deep container – in warm districts. The variety 'World Beater' is a good one.

Radishes, any of the small leaved types like 'Saxa' are easy to grow in containers and so are the white onions for pulling young and green. Even more fun are the cocktail onions which make bulbs of about 1 inch (2·5 cm.)

diameter in 12 weeks. They may of course be pulled smaller and are excellent for boiling with peas and runner beans. The really small bulbs may be used for cocktails.

In warm areas cucumbers may be grown in containers and the white skinned 'White Wonder' or 'Sigmadew', or the green Burpless hybrid are excellent. Many people feel that a cucumber must be green, but 'Sigmadew' is very thin skinned and of excellent flavour. The small apple-shaped cucumber is also worth trying in containers.

A short carrot may be sown in containers and lettuce seedlings planted among the carrots 8 inches (20 cm.) apart. The lettuce will mature first followed by the carrots.

Where there is a fair amount of container space French beans, dwarf broad beans such as 'The Sutton' and even dwarf peas such as 'Little Marvel' may be grown. As indicated above runner beans will also succeed in tubs or large pots. The runner beans, of course, will need strings, a net or some other support up which to climb.

Herbs

All the herbs described on pages 14–15 as being suitable for growing indoors may be grown in containers outdoors and bay trees may be grown to quite large specimens in a tub. Bay trees may, of course, be grown for ornamental purposes, trained as pyramids or as a ball on a stem several feet high. Bay is liable to be damaged in severe winters but may be taken indoors or into a shed or garage during the severest cold spells. The 2 enormous conical bay trees in the garden of the American Embassy in Paris are covered every winter with a fairly close fitting canvas overcoat.

It is probably best, as with herbs in troughs or large containers indoors, to grow the plants in individual pots sunk in peat to prevent rampant plants crowding out the others.

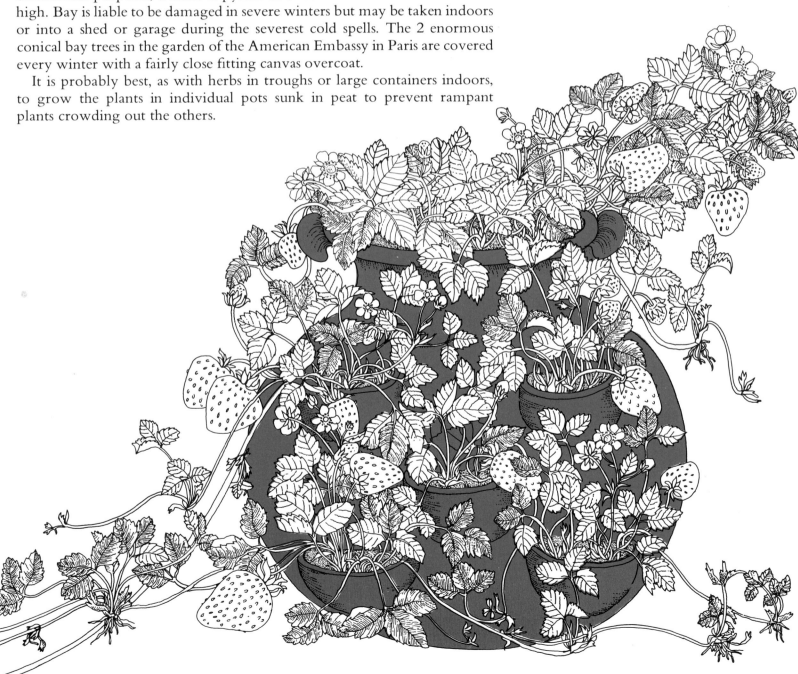

The
Small
Garden

Conditions

We now move on to terra firma as it were because in the past chapters we have been looking at the problems and possibilities of growing plants in window boxes, on balconies, roof gardens and other areas for 'container' planting. Now we have to consider the small back yard or front garden, the terrace or the patio. There may be some soil, or the area may be entirely paved over. Even if an area is paved it is possible that, if desired, some of the paving may be lifted here and there to make a small bed into which a climbing shrub, or even a small tree, could be planted.

Let us first consider the major problems of soil and light, or, more likely, lack of it. The soil in the city, especially if it is many years old, is likely to be thin, dusty, impoverished, devoid of any kind of humus-forming material that will retain moisture, and probably devoid of organic life as well. Soil bacteria are essential as they form a part in the transformation of plant foods into an organic state in which they can be assimilated by the plants. It is usually fairly safe to assume that city soils are acid due to the deposit over many years of acids from the atmosphere.

There are three ways of tackling the problem of city soil. One is to decide to do without it and cover the area if it is small with paving of some kind and then grow plants in containers. There is much to be said for this aspect of city gardening which we will look at in more detail later.

If it is feasible it may be worth while going to the expense of digging up the old soil, or at least part of it in strategic beds or borders, and replacing with fresh good soil from an outside source. This can be, of course, a very expensive operation. However, if the area to be dealt with is not too frightening, this is a good way of dealing with the soil problem.

The third approach would be to set about improving the existing soil, and here it would be necessary either to dig in manure, fresh if possible, if this could be obtained or, failing this, any kind of organic matter, and to give the soil plenty of chemical fertilizers, especially superphosphate, which may be applied up to $1\frac{1}{2}$ ounces (42·5 g.) to the square yard or metre. All this will help to stimulate bacterial activity again.

City soils, too, are liable to be thin and unable to hold moisture well. To assist in moisture retention peat should be dug in as generously as possible, 2–3 pounds (0·9–1·4 kg.) to the square yard, and from about mid-April onwards in the milder climates it would be wise to keep the soil covered with some kind of mulch, peat or spent hops – any organic material that may be available. This will help to conserve moisture in the soil and, important in hot exposed sunny gardens, it will help to keep the roots cool.

Now let us consider the problem of light, or, as is more usual in the city, lack of it. Of course, there will be many gardens, either in front or behind a house, facing due south or west, which will get plenty of sun and if, as often happens, they are surrounded by walls there may be not very much movement of air on hot days and the gardens themselves can become extremely warm. On the other hand there will be gardens with an easterly or northern aspect, or surrounded by other buildings or high walls, into which the sun penetrates possibly only for a short time each day.

There is not much you can do about altering the light factor in a garden except, of course, to paint walls a light colour to help reflect such light as there is and to grow plants that will put up with low light conditions. There are plenty of these, although they may not be the most attractive or desirable plants. The heavily shaded garden is probably at its best in the spring because if part of the shade is cast by trees the early bulbous flowers such as the crocuses, snowdrops, daffodils, and early tulips, muscari, scillas and chiono-doxas, will give their display before the foliage becomes too dense.

It is necessary to differentiate between full sun, partial shade and total shade. With very few exceptions, most of the plants that the amateur wishes to grow in a city garden flourish in full sun. Ferns and hostas are, of course, happier in shade and should not be planted in sunny positions. The great majority of plants that enjoy a fully open position will also give a reasonable account of themselves in partial shade – that is, in a garden or part of a garden which receives some sun for part of each day. Others, which are mentioned elsewhere will do well in a totally shaded position.

Here again, however, we must draw a distinction between shade cast by buildings or distant trees, and that cast by overhanging trees. Many plants do not like to grow in the shade cast by a tree immediately above them, nor do they like the drip of rain from branches of over-hanging trees. These points have to be borne in mind when planning the planting.

Atmospheric pollution is another major problem for the city gardener. In many cities the problem has been controlled and it is now possible to grow almost anything. Where this is not so the golden rule is to grow herbaceous perennials – those that spend the winter underground, bulbs that do the same, deciduous trees and shrubs – those that lose their leaves in the winter – and those often with shiny leaves have demonstrated their ability to survive even in a polluted atmosphere.

There are other hazards inseparable from life in the city. These are the depredations of small children, animals, and birds. All one can do with a front garden is to try to deter children and animals from getting in, using a low fence or hedge possibly of spiny shrubs, such as low growing *Berberis*.

To deter cats getting into back gardens surrounded by a wall or a fence it is sometimes effective if 3–4 strands of loose wire are fixed to the top of the wall or fence. There are also dog and cat repellents to spray in the garden.

Birds, particularly pigeons and sparrows, are a serious problem in the city garden. You can give young seedlings temporary protection by putting hoops of wire netting over them, or covering them with close mesh nylon netting, or even criss-crossing black thread over the plants on sticks 6–8 inches (15–20 cm.) above the ground. This method of stretching black cotton above plants is often used to keep the birds from destroying crocuses, primroses, polyanthus, and other spring flowers.

There are also bird repellent sprays which are often effective in protecting the buds of flowering shrubs and trees, and also fruit bushes, from birds in the winter. It is not claimed that these bird repellents work 100 per cent all the time, but if they are applied, say in mid-November and then again maybe 6–8 weeks later, in areas with a high bird population, you do deter the birds in very many cases.

Having at length listed the hazards of gardening in the city, there is something to be said on the credit side. It is usually warmer than in small towns or villages in the country. The city dweller can confidently hope that his plants will not be struck down by a frost quite so early in the autumn and he may hope to escape those sneaky and damaging late spring frosts.

Furthermore, the chemicals that pollute the atmosphere in the city do at least have an inhibiting effect upon plant disease such as black spot of roses and other troubles. In towns that suffered from serious air pollution it was never necessary to spray plants for such diseases. When the pollution was controlled by, for example, smokeless zones, gardeners had to resort to protecting their plants by spraying against diseases. This, however, is a small price to pay for the blessing of clean air.

In spite of the difficulties, with patience, determination, and a wise choice of plants great pleasure, and some profit, may be had from the city garden.

The Paved Garden

(above) Effective use has been made here of gaps left between the paving stones

(right) An attractively planted terrace

The lawn has become a kind of fixation with many people who will try to achieve a small patch of green in the most unpropitious situations. The city dweller, if he is determined to have his patch of grass, at least starts off with the advantage that the soil in the city is usually acid enough to grow good grass, as one can see in so many city squares and parks. The city dweller has the problem of cutting his little lawn because he possibly has no room for a lawn mower, but if he is prepared to get down on his hands and knees with a pair of shears, good luck to him.

There are, of course, lawn substitutes and vast areas of the lawns in Buckingham Palace gardens, for example, are composed of chamomile. It forms a very close-growing neat sward which does not dry out and turn brown as does grass in hot dry weather. The ordinary chamomile that is raised from seed is a flowering plant and needs to be mown, particularly to keep the plant from shooting up flowering stems. Also, whether you raise chamomile from seed or buy plants, the lawns have to be planted laboriously putting a young piece of chamomile about every 4–5 inches (10–12·5 cm.) apart. Weeds have to be kept under control until the chamomile has covered the area and can do its own job of weed suppression.

There is a non-flowering form of chamomile, 'Treneague', which spreads very rapidly, and with patience you can soon have a small green area which can be walked upon and which needs no cutting, or very little.

In North America chamomile is worth experimenting with, but is not always adapted to the colder or drier areas.

The town dweller would, however, do well to forget the lawn and concentrate on paving over most of the area, leaving perhaps only a few small beds or pockets of soil in which permanent plants may be planted. It will not be too arduous or expensive a job to excavate the soil from these small areas and replace it with good fertile soil.

The holes should be big enough, 6 inches (15 cm.) or more across, to contain a fair amount of soil and, of course, the ground must be excavated to the depth of about a foot (30 cm.), and the hole filled with fertile soil. There are many plants which can be grown in these pockets – thymes, saxifrages, aubrieta, iberis, herbs, or even a few colourful dwarf annuals sown each spring.

No matter what kind of paving is used, old stone paving slabs which can very often be obtained from the local council or building suppliers, or concrete paving which today is made in a wondrous assortment of finishes, it is well worth considering leaving small pockets here and there between the stones into which low growing plants can be inserted to break up the flat expanse of paving.

While some plants will stand a certain amount of traffic, it is not wise to put plants in a position where they will be trodden upon very often.

If you wish to grow rock garden plants, gaps in paving or walls make very useful niches for them, and they often succeed better in such situations than they would in the soil on a rock garden. The reason is that the rain water does not lie around the crown of the plant as it would around plants growing in soil in a rock garden or border, and there is less danger of the crown of the plant rotting.

58

If a garden is shaded, if it is on a slope or on different levels connected by steps; if it is to be used frequently by elderly people who possibly walk with a stick, it is best to avoid stone paving slabs. These may very soon become covered with green slippery algae and can be very dangerous. So, too, can smooth concrete as this may also be covered in autumn and winter with slippery algal growth. In choosing paving slabs keep an eye open for those with a slightly rough surface as these are less likely to become slippery.

Having once paved the garden, patio, terrace or whatever, the annual labour and expense of trying to keep the area of garden soil fertile has been eliminated. You can then concentrate the expenditure upon a variety of attractive containers – genuine stone sinks which may still be found in certain districts although they are fast disappearing, concrete imitation sinks, tubs, fibreglass imitation lead cisterns, troughs, vases, and indeed a whole range of attractive containers in which to grow plants.

Containers are economical both of soil and plants. A few plants hanging down, and a few standing up are often all that is required to create a charming feature.

As mentioned on page 46, containers such as tubs and sinks, whether genuine stone sinks or imitation stone sinks made from concrete, offer the opportunity of growing a wide variety of plants in a small area. Those that require, say, an acid soil can be grown in one container, and those that prefer soil that is rather more limy can be planted in another container. Plants that need a certain amount of shade can be grown together and placed in a shady part of the garden.

The plants mentioned earlier as suitable for growing in tubs and containers are also, of course, all quite suitable for growing in a back yard or patio. Whether in patio or back yard, there is usually more room for plants to grow than on a balcony or on a roof, and a list is appended of shrubs which will succeed well in containers provided these are large enough.

Shrubs for Containers

The following shrubs, or varieties of them, may be grown successfully in large containers:

Aucuba, Berberis, Camellia, Caryopteris, Chamaecyparis, Choisya, Cistus, Clematis, Cotoneaster, Deutzia, Escallonia, Euonymus, Forsythia, Hebe, Hedera, Hydrangea, Hypericum, Jasminum, Kerria, Laurus, Lavendula, Lonicera, Mahonia, Parthenocissus, Passiflora, Pernettya, Prunus, Pyracantha, Ribes, Rosa, Rosmarinus, Spiraea, Syringa, Tamarix Vitis, Weigela, Wistaria.

Naturally shrubs and climbers grown in containers need more care and attention and feeding than their counterparts growing in the ground. Generally speaking shrubs in containers should grow to 4–5 feet (1·2–1·5 m.) high and 3–4 feet (0·9–1·2 m.) across, depending of course on the variety. Climbers should, with proper care and feeding, reach the roof of a 2-storey building.

Plant in a good potting soil – a loam or peat-based mix, with the addition of a general fertilizer according to the maker's instructions. No further feeding should be required in the first year, after which liquid fertilizer should be given regularly to keep growth active and healthy.

Some pruning is obviously necessary to keep shrubs shapely and to restrict growth of the more vigorous types. Root pruning as well as pruning of branches may be necessary after, say 4–5 years. This will entail taking the shrub from its container, and removing the outer layer of soil and roots – say 4–5 inches (10–13 cm.) from the outside of the root ball. Then scrub out the container and replace the shrub, filling it with fresh potting mixture.

60

Plants for Sun and Shade

As mentioned on page 57, most plants will grow in sun or partial shade – that is with sun during some part of the day. There are others that tolerate complete shade, others, like hostas and ferns, that prefer it.

❧ Trees ❧

It is sad that over many years the city dwellers have thoughtlessly planted trees that inevitably grew too large for the space available. The result is a good living for the tree surgeons who have to be called in every few years to cut back these trees – brutally perhaps, but necessarily. Yet it is splendid to plant more trees in towns. There are plenty small enough for many situations, or trees which can be kept small by careful pruning which will not disfigure them.

The smaller cherries, species and varieties of *Prunus*, especially upright varieties like the pink 'Amanogawa', hawthorns, laburnums, catalpas, some magnolias such as *M. soulangeana*, are superb town trees. The robinias, or false acacias, also make excellent town trees as do the crab apples, varieties of *Malus*.

Let us not think that only the small and comparatively short lived trees should be planted in cities. Where there is space for large trees such as limes, or lindens, poplars, oaks, and the plane tree, probably the finest city tree of them all, they should be planted. Many of the more unusual trees flourish in the city – the tulip tree, *Liriodendron tulipifera*, *Paulownia imperialis*, *Cercis siliquastrum*, the Judas tree, varieties of *Gleditschia*, *Cotoneaster frigida*, *Liquidambar styraciflua*, *Koelreuteria paniculata* – all these and many more flourish in the cities largely because they are deciduous. The pines and the spruces – indeed, many evergreen conifers take rather unkindly to smoky cities. Yews, hemlocks and hollies, though, are exceptions among the evergreens.

❧ Shrubs ❧

To learn which shrubs will thrive in your particular city, study your local parks and the mature gardens visible to the passerby.

Again, broadly, except in cities with clean air, concentrate on the deciduous shrubs, taking the risk with evergreens only when you know that local conditions offer a good chance of success.

All the shrubs suggested on the opposite page as suitable for growing in containers may obviously also be grown in beds or borders in the garden. In addition there are some which would not succeed so well in a tub, but are excellent growing in the ground. The butterfly bush, *Buddleia davidii*, in its lilac, reddish purple, purple or white forms, and the exciting *B. alternifolia* are excellent city plants. The latter grown as a standard on a 6–8 foot (1·8–2·4 m.) stem has long 'ropes' of lavender flowers festooning the branches which hang down to the ground.

The *Chaenomeles*, varieties of the Japanese quince, which used to be called *Pyrus japonica*, enjoy the city life; so do varieties of *Philadelphus*, the mock orange, *Viburnum*, *Dipelta* and *Diervilla*.

61

(right) Japanese quince

(far right) *Clematis* 'Nelly Moser'

(below) *Cordyline australis* is the dominant feature of this attractive patio with pelargoniums and fuchsias in the pots in front

In mild areas, most brooms, forms of *Cytisus* and *Genista*, and the yellow Spanish broom, *Spartium junceum*, the hollies, green, golden or silver-variegated, *Skimmia*, and the varieties of *Ulex* or gorse, are worth trying.

Shrubs for Heavy Shade

There are many shrubs that can be grown in heavy shade although they do not necessarily demand it and will grow well in other situations. These, however, are worth a trial in shade – *Aucuba*, *Buxus* (box), *Camellia*, *Elaeagnus*, *Euonymus*, *Fatsia japonica*, *Hypericum*, *Mahonia*, *Prunus lusitanicus*, *Skimmia* and *Viburnum davidii*.

We seize enthusiastically upon south and west facing or protected walls against which we can grow the rather more tender wall shrubs and climbers – also figs, pears, peaches and other fruits. But there are many climbers and wall shrubs that will do well on a north or east facing wall. Good climbers for these cold walls are *Celastrus orbiculatus*, ivies, *Hydrangea petiolaris*, *Parthenocissus* (Virginia creeper) and *Schizophragma hydrangeoides*. Of climbing roses for these less protected walls there is a very wide variety, both the so-called hardy climbers and the more tender climbing hybrid teas if there is enough sun. Some of the best to try are 'Danse du Feu', 'Félicité et Perpétue', 'Gloire de Dijon', 'Hamburger Phoenix', 'Mme Alfred Carrière', 'Mme Caroline Testout', 'Maigold', and 'Paul's Lemon Pillar'.

Shrubs that will grow against north or east walls include *Berberis stenophylla*, *Camellia*, *Chaenomeles*, *Choisya ternata*, *Euonymus fortunei*, *Jasminum nudiflorum*, *Kerria japonica* 'Pleniflora', *Pyracantha* and *Viburnum grandiflorum*.

Ground Cover

The city dweller with limited space to grow plants may feel that he is not making the best use of his ground if he just fills it with permanent ground covering plants. In the larger suburban or country gardens where any help is difficult to find, very expensive, and probably not very knowledgeable when you find it, weed-smothering, labour-saving ground cover plants are almost essential if the garden is not to become a burden.

Even in small town gardens it may be that not much time or labour can be given to the garden, and parts of it, probably under trees or shrubs, can usefully be planted with ground cover.

The ground cover plant par excellence is the ivy in all its forms – green, gold or silver variegated, large or small leaved. It grows under trees or in partial shade; if tree leaves fall on it they may be swished off with a besom or broom, to fall underneath the ivy foliage there to rot and form a nice organic top dressing for the ivy plants.

The periwinkles (*Vinca*), green or variegated, blue or white, are excellent in shade, and so is *Pachysandra terminalis*, but it does not like alkaline or limy soils. The low growing *Hypericum calycinum* does well in sun or shade.

Then there are the various dead nettles, forms of *Lamium*, for sun or shade, but where space is limited *Lamium* 'Chequers', green and white, is a more restrained variety. Other good ground coverers for reasonably sunny areas are *Sedum spectabile* and its varieties, *Veronica gentianoides*, with blue flowers, London pride, and most of the true geraniums, not to be confused with the tender plants generally referred to as geraniums, but more correctly known as varieties of *Pelargonium*, we use for bedding out. Then the epimediums, *Alchemilla mollis* and *Euphorbia robbiae*, are all good ground cover plants.

Most people like to grow a few roses in the garden, but they are not at all attractive for 8 months of the year. So some of the ground cover plants mentioned above, violas or pansies, dwarf bulbs for the spring as well as aubrietas, forget-me-nots and other dwarf flowers that bloom before the roses are very welcome, used to provide interim colour.

If, however, you grow other plants among your roses you must feed the beds or borders rather more generously than you would for roses alone. Give the roses their recommended feeds of a rose vegetable garden fertilizer and supplement this with a granular general fertilizer in the spring, watered in to prevent any danger of scorching the foliage of the ground cover.

Herbaceous Plants

Turning now to herbaceous plants, once again the types that go below ground in winter – that is, whose top growth dies down and is cut off in the autumn – are the most reliable, but others are worth trying in all but the most polluted towns. For early spring we have, besides pansies and English daisies, aubrietas, perennial *Alyssum saxatile*, bergenias, *Helleborus corsicus*, primroses and polyanthus.

A little later come campanulas, aquilegias, oriental poppies, irises, peonies and then the whole galaxy of summer flowers. The phloxes are fine town plants, and should be planted deep, 6–8 inches (15–20 cm.). The campanulas, rudbeckias and heleniums, lilies, *Hemerocallis*, sedums – these and many more do well, including most of those listed below for shade.

When considering plants suitable for growing in shade we have to make a difference between dry shade and moist shade. In a wood there is probably a good depth of moisture-holding organic material, the result of many years of leaves falling and decomposing to form a rich layer of nature's compost. Shady areas in a town are more than likely to be arid areas with thin, dead soil woefully deficient in moisture-holding organic material. Such sites need not be dry as there are plenty of small watering devices as well as permanent and even automatic watering systems that can be installed to keep the areas moist. Naturally it pays handsomely to dig in peat or some other bulky organic material before planting to help conserve the moisture in the soil. Even newspapers soaked and shredded, if dug into the soil, help to hold the moisture.

Some reliable herbaceous perennials for dry shade are *Anaphalis, Epimedium, Euphorbia, Geranium* and *Polygonum*.

For reasonably moist shade there is a much wider choice of herbaceous plants. These include those already mentioned for ground cover, and also *Astilbe, Anemone hybrida* (*A. japonica*), *Filipendula, Hemerocallis, Hosta, Lysimachia, Polygonum, Rodgersia, Thalictrum*, and *Centranthus* (valerian).

Annuals

All the hardy and half-hardy annuals find their place in the town garden, but most need a fair amount of sun. The following, however, will give a good account of themselves in partial shade: annual *Anchusa, Antirrhinum*, begonias, annual *Delphinium, Impatiens* (busy lizzie), *Linaria, Matricaria, Mimulus, Nemophila, Papaver* (poppies), *Salvia*, and *Viola*.

When buying boxes of annual flowers, look suspiciously on those that are already in full flower. This probably means they have been sown and pushed along too early and are already starved in the boxes, which is why they are flowering prematurely; such plants may not be the best buy.

Vegetables

In addition to the vegetables mentioned on page 52 for growing in containers, there are several worth while growing in a bed or border, not only for their crop but for decorative effect. I have mentioned training runner

(following page)
Camellia japonica 'Kimberley'

A collection of ivies – climbing and trailing – add interest to the dimensions of this garden

65

beans against a wall. Another way to grow them, which is very economical of space, is to place a 7–8 foot (2–2·5 m.) pole each side of a garden path so that 6 feet (1·8 m.) of it is above ground. Then bend over a whippy cane or a piece of stout wire into a half circle, and tie each end to the top of a stake.

If pairs of poles are placed about 3 feet (90 cm.) apart, a charming tunnel of greenery, flowers and eventually pods is formed. Grown like this it is not necessary to trample on the ground to pick the beans.

Yet another method is to push in 1–2 stout poles about 6 feet (1·8 m.) apart, and sow or plant a ring of say 10 runner beans around the pole – say about 2 feet (60 cm.) away from the pole. Then tie strings or thin wires to the top of the pole and anchor them firmly, each string alongside a bean plant, tying them to a loop of stout wire or a peg pushed firmly into the ground.

Jerusalem artichokes grow well in towns, and their roots are rather like potatoes. The stems will grow to about 6–7 feet (1·8–2 m.) high and effectively hide an ugly shed or other eyesore.

Globe artichokes are a very different matter. Their leaves are large, deeply cut and very ornamental in a bed or border. Each shoot on a plant will produce three flower heads, which of course are the part of the plant that is eaten. Each year after the first year, in March or April, scrape away the soil and reduce the number of side shoots to three per plant. If more are left the heads will be small. Plant a new row or clump with some of the off-sets. After a plant has cropped for a third year, discard it.

Sweet corn too may be grown in small groups of 2–3 plants in a border of flowers. They are always best grown in a group rather than in a straight line as this ensures pollination no matter which way the wind is blowing.

If you like spinach, the New Zealand spinach makes a large spreading low growing plant which gives masses of fleshy leaves all summer. Seeds may be sown in peat pots indoors in April, or outdoors in early May for planting in late May or early June. This plant is excellent for covering bare ground among other plants provided the site is not too shady.

Rhubarb too will grow well in towns and while not particularly ornamental it is certainly not an eyesore.

Marrows or squashes of the long or trailing variety may be used to cover a rubbish heap. It is best, however, to plant them or sow the seeds at the base of the heap and to allow the plants to ramble up over it. Planted on top of the heap they may not receive enough water.

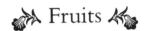

Fruits

All the fruits that can be grown in containers may be grown in the ground, and there are also a few more that are impracticable to grow in containers.

Obviously fruit trees may be grown more successfully in the ground.

An apple, pear or mulberry makes a good shade tree if there is room for it, and a fig, peach, apricot or Morello cherry may be grown against a wall. All, except the Morello cherry, which thrives on an east or north facing wall, need to be grown on a south or west facing wall.

Soft fruits, such as gooseberries, red, white and black currants, thrive in a town. The gooseberries, red and white currants, but not the black currants, may be grown as single, double or triple cordons against a wall or fence, or against canes tied to wires stretched across the garden. This way of growing them is very economical of space and the cordons can be grown to 6 feet (1·8 m.) or more high and carry a very useful crop. However, neither currants nor gooseberries, which serve as alternate hosts, are permitted to be grown in white pine country because of the white pine blister rust.

A few loganberries or cultivated blackberries can be grown against a wall or fence. Alternatively they may be grown against wires stretched between posts and they will form an excellent screen to hide any eyesore. There are thornless loganberries and thornless blackberries and these are the most convenient to grow as they are so easy to prune and tie to their wires.

Raspberries will grow well enough in the city, but they do need full sun and this is not always easy to provide.

Black currants too need an open site, but 3–4 bushes, well grown, will produce a worthwhile crop.

❧ Herbs ❧

All the herbs described as being suitable to grow, indoors or outside, in tubs or other containers may, of course, be grown in beds or borders in a front or back garden. Many of them such as sage, rosemary and bay, may be allowed to grow to their full stature, and do not have to be kept artificially dwarfed by pruning or pinching back.

There are several plants which we can classify as herbs because they have some domestic use but which are also handsome ornamental plants. These include lavender, which may be grown as an individual bush or as a low hedge, and there are over a dozen good varieties. Probably the best all round lavender is 'Munstead' variety, dwarf, dark coloured, growing to about 12 inches (30 cm.) high. Taller, and very free flowering is 'Hidcote' variety. At the other end of the scale are the real dwarfs, excellent for a rock garden or for a pocket in paving.

The bergamots, or varieties of *Monarda*, although invasive, are attractive flowering plants; their leaves when dried are useful mixed with tea.

Fennel makes a handsome tall plant with its finely cut foliage.

Garlic is very easy to grow. Split up a garlic bulb into its segments and plant each one 2 inches (5 cm.) deep and about 6 inches (15 cm.) apart.

The Third Dimension

As city gardens are usually small it is important to make the best use of the third dimension – height. Many attractive plants may be grown against walls or fences, over arches and pergolas, and indeed against screens made of wooden trellis, plastic-covered wire mesh or meshed plastic panels.

There are really only 4 plants which cling to walls or other supports by means of aerial roots – 4, at least, that are commonly found in gardens. These are the ivies in their various colours and forms, virginia creeper, *Hydrangea petiolaris*, the climbing hydrangea, and *Schizophragma hydrangeoides* which is not unlike the climbing hydrangea.

If necessary all of these may be grown in a large tub, but it is best to plant them in the ground even if this means taking up paving to create sufficient space to accommodate the plants, and give them a fair chance of success. It is often thought that plants would object to having their roots covered with concrete or paving, but in fact roots will ramify and flourish.

While these self-clinging climbers are not necessarily the most attractive they are the most trouble free. True, the climbing hydrangea will need a certain amount of clipping back from time to time in order to encourage flowering. Also, if it is allowed to grow out too much from the wall it may

(below) A small pond makes an attractive feature in the corner of this garden

(right) Good use has been made of the third dimension in this garden, ivy is climbing up the rustic pole with the rose 'Iceberg' beneath; runner beans are trained up the wall in the foreground with clematis behind

be blown away from the wall in a fierce gale or by the weight of snow.

Among the other climbers, the most colourful wall plants are, of course, wistaria, climbing roses, clematis and honeysuckles. Colourful too are runner beans – their red flowers contrasting gaily with white or cream walls.

There are various methods of training wall shrubs. The time-honoured method is to drive vine eyes or hooks into the wall – vine eyes are large nails with a hole at the top – and then to thread galvanized, copper or plastic-covered wire horizontally along the wall between the vine eyes. Wires spaced about 2 feet (60 cm.) apart up to a height of about 8 feet (2·5 m.), are usually sufficient to make the training of wall shrubs and climbers easy. A simple method of keeping the wires taut is to thread the wire through the lowest row of vine eyes up to and along the next row and so on until the topmost vine eye is reached. The wire is then made tight to this vine eye and at the bottom a bolt strainer or turnbuckle is fixed between the wire and the lowest vine eye. By tightening up the bolt strainer all the wires are tightened.

Other more expensive but very effective and labour-saving ways are wire panels, preferably plastic-covered panels, which may be fixed to the walls and kept just 1–2 inches (2·5–5 cm.) away from the surface by wiring them to vine eyes or large nails driven into the gaps between the bricks. Where the concrete pointing is very hard it may be necessary to drill holes and plug these before driving in or screwing in the fasteners.

With many types of wall shrubs it is not necessary to tie the shoots to plastic-covered mesh panels as such climbers as honeysuckles will twist themselves in and out of the meshes, clematis will cling to the wires by means of their leaf stalks, and the young growths of climbing roses for example, can be woven in and out of the meshes by hand as they grow.

There are, of course, many shrubs that will grow to a reasonable height, 6 feet (1·8 m.) or more, against walls and which may need no support. The firethorn, or pyracantha, is one and there are others such as forsythias, the flowering currants and *Kerria japonica*; for north walls there are camellias.

Considerable use may be made of arches and pergolas that will give height to a garden and add welcome colour. The arches may be constructed of virtually any material – rustic poles, squared and planed timber, or even of plastic covered wire. The arch itself is not necessarily a thing of great beauty, but it is usually almost obscured when it is covered by a climbing rose, clematis, honeysuckle or other flowering plant.

The introduction of plastic mesh netting and plastic covered wire panels has made the construction of pergolas to provide a shady sitting place in a town garden, very easy. A framework of uprights and 1–2 rafters for the roof is constructed, then the wire mesh panels may be attached to one or more sides and to the roof, thus giving a shelter as well as privacy.

The Russian vine, *Polygonum baldschuanicum* is a great plant for the city, and it grows prodigiously in almost any conditions – indeed, its common name, the mile-a-minute plant, indicates how rapidly it will grow. It is, of course, deciduous, but it makes a fairly thick mass of branches which, even without their leaves, form a useful screen. It may be clipped back as hard as desired with shears each spring. From midsummer until the coming of the frosts it covers itself with billowy white blossoms.

A grape vine does well, or one of the ornamental vines such as *Vitis coignetiae*, with enormous leaves that turn to crimson scarlet in the autumn.

All the plants mentioned can, of course, be grown in tubs, and climbing nasturtiums may also be grown in tubs or containers to climb up a support.

There is often some kind of an eyesore to be screened or camouflaged in a garden. Here again, simple panels of wire mesh fixed between wooden posts or metal uprights form a convenient support for such climbers as sweet peas, honeysuckles, or the Russian vine.

Pools and Flood-Lighting

Separately, or, even better, in combination, these two features can be used to great effect in the tiniest area. A pool opens up the possibilities of growing water plants and also provides a wonderfully cool relaxing atmosphere. Flood-lighting will enhance this, or any other feature of the garden.

Pools

Even the smallest courtyard, patio, or back garden can be greatly enhanced by a small ornamental pool in which 1–2 waterlilies and other aquatic plants may be grown (see p. 41).

If a small fountain is installed, the movement of water and the gentle sound it produces make a pleasant feature of the patio, and if some discreet floodlighting is also installed, the effect is charming.

Small submersible electric pumps may be placed in the pool, and there are models which will automatically give a changing pattern of jets.

Waterproof lighting equipment is available so that you can have an electric light, plain or coloured, submerged in the pool.

As regards the pool itself, we do not today consider digging a hole and building a pool with concrete walls and base. Prefabricated plastic pools may be had in various shapes and sizes, and these are just dropped into a hole of suitable shape and size.

For town gardens, square or rectangular shaped pools are usually the most appropriate. Irregularly shaped pools are more suitable for the more informal settings that you would have in a country garden.

It is often not possible to dig a hole to accommodate a prefabricated pool. In such situations the pool can be set on a brick and concrete base and a low wall of brick or flat stone built around it. If the wall is thick enough, say, a double wall with a cavity of about 15 inches (28 cm.) left between the 2 walls, a flat coping stone may be placed on top of the walls all round the pool, and this makes a useful seat.

When laying an electric cable to the pool – a job for a competent electrician – it is wise to lay a piece of plastic pipe from a mains supply to the pool also, so that the water level can be raised by turning a tap or faucet.

Floodlighting

A garden should be used as an extra room to the house whenever possible, and in a city on a hot evening it is very pleasant to dine or sit outside. Some discreet floodlighting is therefore an asset. This may take the form of a few fixed lights, or a small set of, say, half a dozen lights, plain or coloured, or a mixture of both.

It is possible to buy a kit of half a dozen portable lamps powered by a 12 volt transformer. These may be moved about as required – a lamp which has been illuminating a clump of early tulips can be moved to light up a lilac or some other feature.

Whatever type of lighting is installed, it is essential to specify waterproof equipment suitable for use outdoors, and any mains wiring should be done by a competent electrician.

73

A-Z of Plants

Climatic differences throughout the world affect the range of plants available. Many varieties are available on both sides of the Atlantic; where a variety is particular to a certain country, this is indicated in the text.

Bulbs

Chionodoxa (glory of the snow)
Small starry flowers borne singly or in sprays on slender stems a few inches high, from February to March.
Varieties: *C. luciliae* 'Rosea', rose-coloured, 'Pink Giant', 'Gigantea', violet-blue. Height 6–8 inches (15–20 cm.).
Ordinary soil, including limy; light shade for most intense colours.
Plant in autumn, 2–3 inches (5–7·5 cm.) deep and 4 inches (10 cm.) apart in groups.

Crocus and Colchicum

Chalice-shaped blooms in many colours; certain kinds, particularly autumn-flowering, appear before the leaves. Flowers from early autumn to late spring. Ordinary soil, best in sun or the blooms fail to open fully.
Varieties: *Crocus speciosus* in blue or white, autumn-flowering;
C. chrysanthus varieties: 'Snow Bunting', white, 'Zwanenburg Bronze', bronze with yellow inside petals; 'E. A. Bowles', rich yellow; spring-flowering.
Plant corms in early autumn, 3 inches (7·5 cm.) deep, 6 inches (15 cm.) apart.

Eranthis hyemalis (aconite)

Buttercup-like flowers surmounting a ruff of narrow leaves, February to March. Height 4 inches (10 cm.). One of the first spring bulbs to appear, often in the hardest weather. Any soil, including limy. Shady site best, often naturalizes beneath trees. Plant tubers in late summer, 1 inch (2·5 cm.) deep, 4 inches (10 cm.) apart.

Fritillaria

Pendent bell flowers borne singly on slender arching stems or clustered thickly on upright fleshy stems. Flowers from April to May. Any fertile soil, sun or light shade. Species and varieties: *F. imperialis* (crown imperial), reddish yellow flowers formed in a circular cluster beneath a rosette of glossy green leaves on top of the stem, 2–3 feet (60–90 cm.); *F. meleagris* (snakeshead), solitary or paired flowers on thin stems; petals chequered many shades: 'Aphrodite', white, 'Saturnis', violet-red, 'Poseidon', purple-spotted. Plant bulbs in autumn, 4–6 inches (10–15 cm.) deep. The crown imperial should be an inch (about 2·5 cm.) or so deeper. Leave plants undisturbed or they may not flower well.

Galanthus (snowdrop)

Bright little winter-flowering bulbs. Flowers are made up of 2 sets of petals: 3 long ones and 3 inner short ones; blooms nodding on short slender stems among narrow leaves. Species and varieties: *G. elwesii*, bluish leaves, inner petals deep green; *G. nivalis*, common snowdrop; *G. nivalis* 'Flore-plena' has double flowers; 'S. Arnott' is much taller with large single blooms.

Fritillaria meleagris

Good in shade or sun, ordinary soil,
thrive on limy.
Increase plants by dividing clumps
after flowering, before the leaves
disappear, and replanting pieces 6
inches (15 cm.) apart.

Hyacinthus
Sturdy spikes of flared and starry
tubular flowers, in shades of blue, red,
pink, white and yellow. Height 6–8
inches (15–20 cm.). Best in fertile soil;
sun or light shade. Blooms appear
from December to May.
Varieties: 'City of Haarlem', yellow;
'Delft Blue', light blue; 'Jan Bos', red.
Roman hyacinths have looser spikes
of bloom with fewer flowers in white,
pink or blue.
Plant 5–6 inches (13–15 cm.) deep in
early autumn for flowering in spring.

Iris
The flowers comprise 3 upright petals
– the standards – and 3 broad lip-
shaped petals – the falls. Narrow
leaves arise from the base of the plant.
Ordinary soil, sun or light shade.
Plants do well in limy areas.
Species and varieties: *I. reticulata*, small
rock-garden kind in deep blue with an
orange blotch; plant 2–3 inches (5–7·5
cm.) deep.
Hybrids: Dutch, Spanish and English.
Dutch kinds in white, yellow, blue or
purple, flower from early to mid June.
2 feet (60 cm.).
Spanish: flower 2 weeks later and come
in many attractive shades. 18 inches
(45 cm.).
English: late flowering – in July –
white, pink, blue or purple. Only
yellow is missing from the colour
range.
Plant bulbs 4 inches (10 cm.) deep and
6 inches (15 cm.) apart in early autumn.

Lilium (lily)
Flared trumpet- or chalice-shaped
blooms in many colours. Flowers
borne on slender stems clothed with
narrow glossy green leaves. Most
lilies prefer light shade and a cool root
run, ideally among other shrubs which
can support them as they grow up and
between them. Heights from 2–6 feet
(60 cm.–1·8 m.).
Species and varieties: *L. auratum
rubrum*, white red-striped petals; *L.
candidum*, pure white trumpet blooms;
L. tigrinum, turk's cap bloom in orange
red with black spots; Bellingham
Hybrids, orange, red, yellow and

bicolours, all marked with brown
spots.
Planting depth depends on the habit of
the plant. For example, *L. candidum*
is set 2 inches (5 cm.) deep, *L.
tigrinum*, 6 inches (15 cm.), *L.
auratum*, 6–12 inches (15–30 cm.).
Those set deeply are stem rooting and
others set shallowly are basal rooting.

Muscari (grape hyacinth)
Clusters of narrow green leaves and
tightly packed cones of bloom, except
for *Muscari comosum* 'Plumosum'
which has feathery tassel flowers.
Any soil, sun or quite deep shade.
Perfect edging plant, completely
hardy, multiplies freely.
Varieties: *M. armeniacum*, pale blue,
'Heavenly Blue', bright blue. Height
8 inches (20 cm.). *M. comosum* (as
above in clear sky blue); *M.
tubergenianum*, light and dark blue
flowers clustered on the same spike.
Height 8 inches (20 cm.).
Plant bulbs in late summer and
autumn, 3 inches (7·5 cm.) deep, 6
inches (15 cm.) apart.

Narcissus (daffodil)
Broad or narrow, trumpet or tubular
flared blooms in yellows and whites.
For borders, woodland, or rock
gardens. Best in well-worked soil in
sun or light shade. Good for
brightening gloomy spots. From 2
inches to 2 feet (5–60 cm.).
Species and varieties: *N. bulbocodium*
(the hoop coat daffodil), circular,
flared yellow trumpets; 'Golden
Harvest', deep yellow trumpet;
'Mount Hood', white trumpet; 'Ice
Follies', yellow cup with white petals;
'Mary Copeland', double pinkish
white ruffled petals, orange centre;
'Actaea', the pheasant's eye, pure white
petals with bright orange cupped
centre.
Plant in autumn for flowering in
spring. Set bulbs to 3 times their depth
in the soil.

Raise new plants from old clumps by
splitting up bulb clusters after flowering.

Tulipa (tulip)
Single, double or flared chalice-shaped
blooms for many weeks in late winter
and spring. Ordinary soil in sun or
light shade.
Varieties: among the botanical tulips,
reddish starry bloomed *T.
kaufmanniana* 'Shakespeare', yellow,
flushed-red *T. clusiana*, *T. chrysantha*,
and scarlet *T. praestans* 'Fusilier', are
outstanding. Heights around 12 inches
(30 cm.). The single early tulips such
as orange-red 'Couleur Cardinal',
white 'Diana' and 'Pink Perfection'
have narrow chalice blooms. Heights
from 6–15 inches (15–38 cm.).
Completely different are the double
late tulips. Resembling full double
peony blooms, red 'Brilliant Fire',
deep yellow 'Gold Medal' and white
'Mount Tacoma' are magnificent.
Heights about 18 inches (45 cm.).
Raise plants from bulbs set 3 times
their depth in the soil in autumn and
early winter.

Biennials

Bellis (double daisy)
Bright little pompon flowers are borne
on 6 inch (15 cm.) stems from May to
June. Sun or semi-shade, ordinary soil.
Varieties: 'Colour Carpet', shades of
red, pink and white; F_1 hybrid 'Fairy
Carpet', rose or white double flowers;
'Pomponette Pink Buttons', quilled
petals forming dainty ball heads in
shades of rose or pink.
Raise plants from seed sown in a
nursery bed in May. Plant out
seedlings when they are large enough
to handle and set 6 inches (15 cm.)
apart where they are to flower.

Campanula medium (Canterbury
bells)
Large single or double bell-shaped
blooms set in huge clusters on sturdy
stems. Ordinary soil, sun or light shade.
Varieties: the single types such as
'Bells of Holland', blue-mauve, rose or
white blooms on 15 inch (38 cm.)
stems; Cup and Saucer varieties with
semi-double blooms: often offered as
Pure White, Deep Rose-Pink, Blue
and Special Mixture.
Either sow in gentle heat in late
winter to flower in summer, or raise
plants in June, in light shade to have
them flowering the following spring.

Cheiranthus cheiri (wallflower)
Dense spikes of gaily coloured blooms
in spring and early summer. Ordinary
soil, including limy in which they are
less liable to contract club root disease
which can cripple growth. Sun or
light shade.
Varieties: 'Giant Blood Red', 'Giant
Yellow', 'Giant Fire King', scarlet,
all 18 inches (45 cm.) high; 'Persian
Carpet', cream, apricot, rose, purple
and many other shades of flowers on 15
inch (38 cm.) stems, perfect for
bedding and spreading.
Raise plants from seed sown in May in
a nursery bed. Plant out seedlings 4
inches (10 cm.) apart to grow on for
finally transplanting to their flowering
positions in early autumn, to bloom in
spring.

Dianthus barbatus (sweet william)
Massed auricula-type blooms in huge
clusters on short stems. Sun or light
shade, ordinary soil, including limy.
Varieties: both Single and Double
Mixed as well as single colours in
many shades of salmon, scarlet and
purple, each flower having distinctive
white eye. Heights from 6–18 inches
(15–45 cm.).
Grow as an annual, raising plants early
in spring to flower the same year, or as
a biennial, sowing seed in June to get
plants flowering the following early
summer.

Myosotis (forget-me-not)
Intense, mostly blue, flowers in sprays
or clusters on short stems. Perfect for
interplanting with tulips.
Sun or light shade. Ordinary soil,
including limy in which they thrive.
Varieties: 'Royal Blue', 12 inches
(30 cm.); 'Bouquet', 'Indigo Blue',
10 inches (25 cm.); 'Carmine King',
8 inches (20 cm.); 'Miniature Blue',
ball-shaped flower clusters, 5 inches
(13 cm.), ideal for edging.
Raise plants in June for flowering the
following May to July.

Primula vulgaris (polyanthus)
Vivid-hued primrose-like flowers
borne in huge semi-circular clusters
on short thick stems. Ordinary soil
best enriched with plenty of old
manure to encourage sturdy growth
and fine flowers; will tolerate limy
soil. Light shady position to prevent
flowers being burnt up by the sun; this
also prolongs the display.
Varieties: 'Triumph' Strain, huge

blooms, around 2 inches (5 cm.)
across in white, yellow, pink, red and
blue shades; 'Pacific Dwarf Jewel'
Strain, plants only 7 inches (18 cm.)
high, wide range of colours; 'Suttons'
Giant' Strain, many brilliant hues,
plants tough and weather resistant.
Heights of all varieties range from
6–9 inches (15–23 cm.).
Raise plants from seed sown in gentle
heat in late winter or early spring.
Prick out seedlings in trays of good
soil and harden them off before
setting them outdoors in early
autumn where they are to flower.
Birds peck at yellow-petalled varieties,
so you may find that black netting or
thread may have to be strung over the
plants.

Viola tricolor or **V. x wittrockiana**
(pansy)
Low growing spreading plants massed
with open almost circular, plain or
'faced' blooms in many colours.
Ordinary soil in full sun for finest
flowers. Varieties: 'Roggli Giant'
strains – 'Alpengluhn', red, 'Jungfrau',
creamy white, 'Eiger', yellow with
black blotch, 'Thunersee', blue.
Raise plants in summer for planting
out in autumn to bloom the following
spring. Alternatively, sow seed in
February or March to bloom the
same year.

V. hybrida (viola)
Smaller blooms than pansies, freer
flowering, compact plants.
Many and varied varieties.
Raise plants as for pansies, above.

Hardy Annuals

Calendula (marigold)
Orange, yellow or creamy, single or
double large daisy-like flowers, 2½–4
inches (6–10 cm.) across. Ordinary
soil. Full sun. Thrive without special
care.
Varieties: 'Orange Coronet', 1 foot

(30 cm.), golden orange; 'Dwarf
Golden Gem', 10 inches (25 cm.),
golden yellow; 'Happy Talk' mixed,
2 feet (60 cm.), lemon, yellow-gold
and orange; 'Double Art Shades', 2
feet (60 cm.), soft cream to deep
yellow.
Raise new plants from seed sown
indoors or outdoors in situ; thin
plants to 6–8 inches (15–20 cm.) apart.

Centaurea cyanus (cornflower)
Narrow upright plant with tapering
leaves and stems topped by double
pompon-like flowers, blue, pinkish or
white.
No special soil, best in full sun,
though will tolerate light shade.
Support plants with small twigs in
windy districts. Discard after
flowering.
Raise new plants from seed sown
outdoors in spring when frosts over or
indoors earlier.

Clarkia
Erect stems clustered with rounded
blooms in many colours. Best in full
sun, happy in ordinary soil which, if
slightly poor, induces better flowering.
Varieties: *C. pulchella* mixed, 1 foot
(30 cm.), semi-double flowers in
white, violet, carmine rose and other
shades. Good cut flower.
Raise new plants from seed sown in
situ outdoors in spring when soil
workable. Also makes a good pot
plant for conservatory or greenhouse.
In sheltered areas, sow in autumn,
cover plants in severe weather and
look forward to earlier flowering
plants in summer.

Godetia
Flamboyant, flared, cup-shaped
blooms in vivid colours, borne in
masses on short stems. Thrives in
ordinary soil, best in full sun. May also
be grown in pots for flowering
indoors.
Varieties: 'Scarlet Emblem', 15 inches
(38 cm.), rich crimson-scarlet;
'Monarch Dwarf Bedding', 1 foot
(30 cm.), rainbow-hued blooms, single
flowered; 'Sybil Sherwood', 1 foot
(30 cm.), pinkish orange.
Raise plants from seed sown in situ
outdoors in spring; for earlier flowers
sow in September but cover with
cloches if weather severe.

Lathyrus odoratus (sweet pea)
Flowers in red, pink, maroon, blue,

cream, lavender and many other shades, including picotees in rich cream with deep rose frilly edged petals. Heights vary from 12–18 inches (30–45 cm.), to 6–8 feet (1·8–2·4 m.). Best in deep fertile soil in full sun.

Varieties: among the free flowering, vigorous Spencer varieties are white 'Swan Lake', cerise 'Percy Izzard', scarlet 'Air Marshal' and mid-blue 'Noel Sutton'.

Jet Set varieties are about 3 feet (90 cm.) high but are as prolific as the taller kinds. 'Blue Naples', salmon, cream-pink 'Killarney' and scarlet 'Madrid' are superb. Knee-Hi varieties carry sturdy stems of 5–10 blooms in a mixture of colours and are splendid for window boxes. Where scent is important, this is provided by a group called 'Old-fashioned Scented' mixed. Flowers are fairly small in comparison to the others mentioned, but more than compensate by their richness of scent. Raise plants in autumn and over-winter in a cold frame, planting out in spring, or sow in situ in spring. Insert twiggy sticks to support plants or grow them up canes and pinch out their side shoots and tendrils. Huge flowering stems develop on these specially trained cordon plants.

Linaria (toad flax)
Snapdragon-like flowers in dainty spikes around 9 inches (23 cm.) high. Blooms in many colours including violet, blue, crimson, pink and yellow. Ordinary soil in sun or light shade.

Variety: 'Fairy Bouquet', a colourful mixture. Shear off faded flowers to encourage more to grow in late summer and early autumn.

Raise plants from seed sown in situ in spring. Thin to 3–4 inches (7·5–10 cm.) apart.

Malcolmia (Virginia stock)
Slender stemmed plants carrying heads of cruciform flowers around ½ inch (1·3 cm.) across. They are sweetly scented and bloom for several weeks.

Will grow almost anywhere but thrive in full sun.

Varieties: *M. maritima* mixed, in various colours – red, lilac, rose or white; 'Nana Compacta', a dwarf form, again in several shades. Height around 8 inches (20 cm.).

Raise plants from seed sown in March and successively at monthly intervals to give flowers over a long period. September sowing gives plants for overwintering and flowering early the following spring.

Phacelia campanularia
Gorgeous upturned gentian blue-bell flowers borne on 9 inch (23 cm.) stems. One of the really true blue annuals. Flowers for most of the summer and these attract bees. Best in full sun; ordinary soil.

Raise plants from seed sown in situ in spring. Space plants to 6 inches (15 cm.) apart.

Fuchsia 'Snowcap'

Reseda (mignonette)
Tall thin spikes of sweetly scented
flowers. Beloved by bees, this fragrant
annual is best planted close to the
house where its scent can waft through
open windows. Thrives in full sun in
ordinary soil and limy areas.
Varieties: 'Suttons' Giant', 12 inches
(30 cm.), ideal for pots, very fragrant;
'Sweet-Scented', a 15 inch (38 cm.)
high variety of great merit. Flowers of
all varieties greenish yellow, except
'Machet', golden yellow and 'Red
Monarch', red and green.
Raise plants from seed sown in situ in
March. Thin to 6 inches (15 cm.)
apart.

Tropaeolum (nasturtium)
Carpeting or trailing plants with
distinctive rounded leaves and showy
flared trumpet flowers, often with
short spurs. Thrive in ordinary soil,
the less fertile the better, or too many
leaves appear and swamp the few
flowers that form. Fine plant for tubs,
window boxes or for climbing over
trellis-work.
Varieties: 'Golden Gleam', 'Scarlet
Gleam', 'Cherry Rose' (dwarf double).
The canary flower, *Tropaeolum
canariense* (*T. peregrinum*), is a vigorous
climber whose leafy stems are massed
with exotic looking clear yellow

flowers with shaped and frilled petals.
Raise plants from seed where they are
to flower. Provide netting or trellis for
the climbing forms, which also trail.

Viscaria (syns *Lychnis*, *Silene*)
Slender stems topped by single pink-
like flowers in pink, red, blue or white.
Ordinary soil in full sun, though will
grow well in limy areas.
Varieties: 'Sutton's Brilliant' mixture;
'Nana Compacta' mixed, delightful
colour range: flowers borne on low
growing plants 6–9 inches (15–23 cm.)
high. Grow as a massed display for
effect.
Raise plants from seed sown outdoors
in spring; thin to 6 inches (15 cm.) apart.

Summer Bedding

Ageratum
Fine edging or carpeting plant massed
with thickly clustered bobble flowers
on 5–9 inch (13–23 cm.) stems. Good
for sun or light shade in ordinary soil.
Varieties: F_1 hybrid 'Blue Blazer', F_1
hybrid 'Summer Snow', 'Little Blue
Star' and reddish-blue 'Blue Mink'.
Raise plants in gentle heat in late
winter or early spring. Prick out
seedlings into seed boxes, harden them
off and plant outdoors in late spring or
when frosts are over.

Phacelia campanularia

Alyssum (now *Lobularia maritima*)
Effective edging plant with spreading
clusters of tiny flowers. Also grows on
walls or between crazy paving.
Ordinary soil, sun or light shade.
Varieties: white 'Little Dorrit',
'Carpet of Snow'; rose-pink, 'Rosie
O'Day', 'Lilac Queen'.
Sow in spring where plants are to
flower and thin seedlings to 4 inches
(10 cm.) apart, or start indoors and
transplant for early bloom.

Antirrhinum (snapdragon)
Showy spikes of tubular lipped
flowers. Full sun, ordinary soil.
Types: Carpet (6–8 inches, 15–20 cm.);
Bedding (16 inches, 40 cm.); Giant
Tetraploid (28 inches, 70 cm.);
Butterfly or Penstemon–flowered (30
inches, 75 cm.); Double (36 inches,
90 cm.); Rocket (36 inches, 90 cm.)
all with wide varieties of colour.
Raise plants from seed sown indoors
with gentle heat in late winter or early
spring. Prick out seedlings in seed
trays of potting mix and harden
them off ready for planting outdoors
in late May or early June or plant
outdoors directly when soil is
workable.

Shear off first flush of blooms when they fade, to encourage flowering side shoots.

Begonia semperflorens (bedding begonia)
Glossy rounded bright green, coppery or purplish leaves and thick clusters of red, pink or white flowers from late spring to early autumn. Sun or semi-shade. Ordinary soil. Water freely and feed well for strong flowering shoots.
Varieties: F_1 hybrid 'Bella', carmine-rose; 'Fireball', carmine-scarlet with puckered leaves; 'Snowball', white, green leaves; 'Pink Comet', salmon-pink; (North America only, 'Red Planet', 'Northern Lights').
Plant out for summer display when frosts are over. Dig up some plants in autumn, overwinter in a frost-free place and take cuttings of the young shoots in early spring. Alternatively, raise plants from seeds.

Callistephus (China aster)
Floppy chrysanthemum-like blooms all summer. Best in full sun in ordinary soil.
Types: Carpet (8 inches, 20 cm.); Cactus; Powderpuff; Full Double; Super Giant semi-formal; all with wide varieties of colour.
Raise plants from seeds sown with gentle heat indoors in spring. Prick out seedlings in shallow trays and harden them off before setting outdoors in late May to flower from June onwards or sow outdoors as soon as soil conditions permit.

Dahlia
Flowers in many shades of colour. They highlight late summer with their brilliant hues, continuing until cut down by frost in autumn. There are several classic shapes; blooms can

range from 4–10 inches (10–25 cm.) across.
Single-flowered – consisting of an outer ring of petals and a large yellow boss in the centre.
Anemone flowered – blooms like anemones.
Collerette – ring of tubed petals overlapping outer ring of flat spoon-shaped petals.
Peony flowered – flowers consist of 2 or more circles of flattened petals.
Decorative: magnificent double flowers subdivided into Giants, with 10 inch (25 cm.) blooms, large, medium, small, miniature.
Ball – ball-shaped blooms.
Pompon – similar to ball-flowered dahlias but with smaller and more globular flowers.
Cactus – sharply quilled petals.
There are hundreds of varieties in almost every shade imaginable. Best in full sun though will tolerate light shade. Ordinary soil enriched with old manure to prolong the display.
Raise plants from seeds, tubers, or cuttings.

Dianthus chinensis (Indian pink)
Vivid-hued blooms, single or double in self or mixed colours. Full sun. Thrive in most soils, particularly those rich in lime.
Varieties: 'Baby Doll', single flowers, many brilliant shades, petals attractively patterned, 6 inches (15 cm.); *D. heddewigii* 'Fireball', glorious scarlet, 9 inches (23 cm.); (North America: 'Snowflake', single, white).
Pinch out growing points to encourage bushiness and plenty of flowers.
Raise plants with gentle heat indoors in late winter or early spring. Prick off seedlings in shallow trays of gritty compost, harden off and plant outdoors in late May or early June or sow directly outside when soil permits.

Fuchsia
Tubular ballet-skirted flowers borne along slender arching shoots. Plants hardy or tender. Blooms brighten late summer and early autumn. Heights from 2 inches (5 cm.) with the carpeting form of *F. procumbens*, to 8 feet (2·4 m.) or more and as much across with *F. magellanica*. Best in deep fertile soil in light shade, though will tolerate full sun. Coloured leaved varieties best in good light.

Some hardy varieties. Most, however, make excellent bedding subjects but must be overwintered in a frost-free greenhouse: 'Texas Longhorn', large double red and white flowers; 'White Spider', gorgeous slender petalled flowers.
Prune back flowered shoots to within a few inches of the main framework in spring, to encourage sturdy new flowering shoots.
Raise new plants from seed or cuttings.

Heliotrope (cherry pie)
Clusters of small deeply coloured flowers top stems set with broadly spear-shaped, deeply veined leaves, 12–18 inches (30–45 cm.) high. Ordinary soil in good light, but will tolerate light shade. Stake plants in windy districts.
Varieties: deep blue 'Marina'; violet-blue 'Lemoine's Giant'. All have a strong sweet scent. Can be grown as standards. Best sown in gentle heat in February or March, pricked out to grow on strongly and set outdoors in late May or early June to flower throughout the summer.
Increase plants from seed, or cuttings taken in September and kept growing steadily in a frost-free greenhouse throughout the winter.

Impatiens (busy lizzie)
Bright flattish or cup-shaped flowers borne singly or in small clusters on fleshy stems. Height, 6 inches (15 cm.) to 2 feet (60 cm.). Ordinary soil, in sun or light shade.
Come in a wide variety of colours including light pink, rose, plum, scarlet, salmon, tangerine and white; some with variegated leaves. New are Elfin Series and fancy-leaved sorts. Raise new plants from seed or cuttings. Frost-tender.

Lobelia
Tiny broad-lipped tubular flowers borne in immense numbers on spreading or trailing stems. Excellent edging plant for borders or window boxes. Any good soil, sun or light shade.
Varieties: *L. erinus* 'Blue Gown', sky-blue; 'Mrs Clibran Improved', deep blue with a white eye; 'White Lady'; 'Rosamund', carmine-red; 'Sapphire', azure-blue, with distinctive white eye, good trailing variety.
Raise plants in gentle heat and bed them out for the summer when frosts

are over or sow outdoors directly for later blooming.

Lobularia maritima, see Alyssum

Nicotiana (tobacco plant)
Tubular blooms, richly fragrant, borne in large numbers atop slender stems. Ideal for sun or light shade in any soil.
Varieties: 'Evening Fragrance', petunia-like flowers in many shades emit superb fragrance, especially at dusk, 3 feet (90 cm.); 'Affinis', pure white, very fragrant, 32 inches (80 cm.); 'Dwarf Idol', bright crimson; 'Lime Green' or 'Lime Sherbet', flowers of that colour; 'Sensation' mixed, many colours, and blooms remain wide open in daylight.
Raise new plants from seeds sown in gentle heat in late winter and planted outdoors in June or when frosts are over.

Pelargonium (geranium)
Mostly round-headed clusters of single or double flowers, with plain or frilled petals. Foliage particularly attractive in the zonal and ivy-leaved varieties. Good rich soil, full sun or light shade. All groups include a wide selection of colours.
Types: Best known are the zonals, so called because their leaves are zoned or patterned: come in a wide selection of varieties and colours, also miniatures.
Regal or 'Martha Washington' pelargoniums: less hardy and floriferous than the zonals; waved or crinkled leaves.
Scented geraniums with leaves of varied fragrances.
Ivy geraniums: perfect for cascading from tubs or window boxes. Care-free strain, a group more readily grown from seed for use the same year.
Overwinter bedded-out geraniums from October onwards in a frost-free greenhouse, a cold room or store in their soil in a cellar. Take cuttings in August. Again keep them growing through the winter in a cool, but frost-proof place.

Petunia
Very showy, single or double saucer-shaped flowers borne on short stems that spread freely in sun or shade. Ordinary soil, best enriched with old manure to prolong flowering.
All colours, singles and doubles, plain-petalled and frilled, dwarf or tall.
Raise plants in gentle heat in winter and, after hardening them off, plant them out for blooming throughout the summer. Propagate doubles by cuttings taken before frost.

Tagetes (French and African marigold)
Single, daisy-like blooms or double, carnation-like blooms are borne freely on short stems from June to late autumn, or as soon as nights grow cold. Ordinary soil in sun or semi-shade.
Types: single, double and anemone-flowered; yellow, orange, brown and two-toned; 4–18 or 20 inches (10–45 or 50 cm.).
Raise plants from seeds sown in gentle heat in late winter or spring and, after pricking off seedlings and hardening them off, plant them where they are to flower, in late May or early June.

Herbaceous plants

Acanthus (bear's breeches)
Handsome with large, deep green leaves and upright flower spikes of hooded blooms from July to August. Ordinary soil, sun or semi-shade.
Species: *A. mollis*, 4 feet (1·2 m.) high, leaves roughly heart-shaped with wavy edges, flowers white and purple; *A. spinosus*, 3–4 feet (90 cm.–1·2 m.) high, long narrow finely cut leaves, white and purple flowers offset by green bracts. Both species bear their flowers on 18 inch (45 cm.) spikes. Shorten stems back to near ground level after flowering.
Raise new plants by dividing the clump in autumn or spring. Take root cuttings or sow seeds.

Aubrieta (rock cress)
Carpeting plant with small silver greyish green leaves and tiny flowers that completely cover the shoots in spring and early summer. Ideal for growing in full sun in poorest soil, between crazy paving, cascading from walls or on a rock garden. Grows well in limy soil. Height 4 inches (10 cm.), spread several feet.
Colours: purple, lavender, white, reddish. Cut back flowered stems when blooms fade to keep plant compact. Top dress crowns with rich gritty soil to boost strong growth.
Raise new plants from cuttings or seeds.

Campanula (bellflower)
Striking open, starry or tubular bell-flowered plants which bloom from spring to late autumn. Sun, semi-shade. Ordinary soil, best if lime added where it is light and sandy.
Herbaceous kinds: *C. lactiflora*, 5 feet (1·5 m.), immense spikes of blue cup-shaped flowers; *C. glomerata* 'Superba', the clustered bellflower, violet bells, does well in shade.
Bedding kinds: *C. medium*, Canterbury bells – 'Bells of Holland', large bell-shaped blooms in pink, blue, white or mauve shades, 15 inches (38 cm.).
Alpine kinds: *C. garganica*, deep blue, mats, 3 inches (7·5 cm.); *C. portenschlagiana* 'Major', violet mauve, 6 inches (15 cm.), excellent for dry walls.
Raise new plants from seeds or rooted offsets of parent clump.
Raise biennial kinds every year, in late spring and plant out in autumn for flowering the following year.

Cineraria maritima (syn. *Senecio cineraria*)
Excellent foliage plant with silvery white, finely cut leaves. Height 2 feet (60 cm.). Small yellow flowers borne in late summer. Sun or light shade, ordinary soil. Fine plant for growing in tubs. Pinch out growing tip to make plant bush out.
Take cuttings in August and over-winter them in a cold frame for planting out the following late spring and early summer.
Prune away faded flower stems and trim to shape. Remove straggly stems when necessary.

Convallaria (lily-of-the-valley)
Spreading, ground-covering plant about 9–12 inches (23–30 cm.) high. Sprays of small white bell-shaped flowers, richly scented, broadly spear-shaped leaves. Blooms in April and May. Ordinary soil, including limy. Sun or quite deep shade.
Flowers white or faintly pink-tinted.
Varieties: *C. majalis*, the common lily-of-the-valley.
Raise new plants from rhizomes dug up in autumn and planted 4 inches (10 cm.) apart, just below the soil surface.

Erigeron (fleabane)
Imposing daisy-like flowers for sun or light shade, mid to late summer. Ordinary soil.
Varieties: 'Foerster's Liebling', 2 feet (60 cm.), semi-double pink; also lavender-blue and violet-blue varieties. Trim off dead flowers occasionally to encourage new blooms.
Raise new plants from rooted offsets of established clumps.

Euphorbia (spurge)
Easy growing perennial for sun or deep shade in ordinary soil, including limy areas. Flowers, actually bracts, are usually well coloured in shades of yellow or green. Leaves handsome, especially in *Euphorbia wulfenii*.
Species and varieties: *E. epithymoides*, saffron-yellow flower heads, spring, early summer. 1 foot (30 cm.);
E. wulfenii, bold clusters of bloom held like clubs on long fleshy stems above stems massed with narrow blue-green leaves; *E. griffithii* 'Fireglow' has flame-coloured bracts; *E. myrsinites*, sun lover for hot spots in dry soil; trailing stems clustered with blue-grey leaves.
Increase plants by splitting up the

Campanula persicifolia

rootstock and setting out rooted portions in autumn or spring.

Grasses (annual and perennial kinds)
Easy, trouble-free plants for admiring in the border or for drying and arranging in the home. Ordinary soil, best in sun.
Annuals: *Briza maxima*, nodding heads, 1½ feet (45 cm.); *Coix lachryma-jobi*, 2½ feet (75 cm.); *Lagurus ovatus* (hare's tail), 1 foot (30 cm.).
Perennials: *Cortaderia selloana* (pampas grass), 5 feet (1·5 m.), towering plumes;
Acorus gramineus variegatus, 8–10 inches (20–25 cm.), narrow leaves striped silver;
Helictotrichon sempervirens, upright blue tufts, 2 feet (60 cm.);
Miscanthus sinensis gracillimus, 5 feet (1·5 m.), blue-green leaves turning yellowish in autumn.
Raise new plants from seed or divisions of older plants.

Helleborus
Generally open cup-shaped flowers on

short stems with sometimes quite striking sculptured leaves. Sun or deep shade. Ordinary soil, grows well in limy. Evergreen leaves.

Species: *H. niger* (Christmas rose), 1 foot (30 cm.) high, bright white flowers in winter; *H. orientalis* (Lenten rose), white, pink or purplish flowers, 1–2 feet (30–60 cm.) high, several to a stem; *H. corsicus*, 3 feet (90 cm.) architectural leaves, light green flowers in clusters.

Raise new plants from seeds or pieces from established clumps.

Heuchera (coral flower)

Massed panicles of tiny bell flowers borne on slender stems among deep green heart- shaped leaves, from June to September. Good in full sun or light shade; leaves make a weed suppressing carpet. Ordinary soil. Colours: red, rose and pinks. *Heucherella* is a bi-generic hybrid between *Tiarella* and *Heuchera* and is vigorous with plentiful sprays of light pink flowers from May to October; flowers longest in light shade. Raise new plants by dividing clumps into rooted pieces.

Hosta (plantain lily)

Superb foliage plant for sun or deep shade. Leaves mostly spear-shaped, bright green, bluish, margined with silver or yellow striped. Best in moist soil. Bold flower spikes of lily-like flowers appear in summer.

Species and varieties: *H. albo-marginata*, lilac flowers, white-edged leaves; *H. fortunei*, fresh green leaves, heliotrope flowers; *H. sieboldiana*, blue-green leaves, effectively crimped, whitish flowers. All grow around 2 feet (60 cm.) high.

Protect succulent shoot tips in spring by baiting against slugs.

Raise new plants by splitting up clumps.

Iberis (candytuft)

Cushions of bloom amid lustrous deep green leaves – a spectacle in spring. Ordinary soil, sun or light shade. Annuals: *I. umbellata*, white, some rose or lavender-tinted.

Perennials: *I. gibraltarica*, flowers opening pink and turning to white; *I. sempervirens*, bright white flowers, evergreen leaves.

Increase plants from seeds or softwood cuttings.

Nepeta (catmint)

Silver-grey leaves attractive all summer and autumn, flowers lavender-blue, in spikes 1–3 feet (30–90 cm.) high. Full sun, ordinary soil.

Species and varieties: *N. mussinii*, 1½ feet (45 cm.), 'Six Hills', 3 feet (90 cm.) darker coloured flowers, vigorous. Perfect edging plant. Leave foliage all winter for its silvery effect. Raise new plants from rooted offsets taken in autumn or spring.

Penstemon

Sprays of snapdragon-like flowers borne in sprays in late spring and early summer. Ordinary soil, sun or light shade.

Varieties: 'Firebird', scarlet, 3 feet (90 cm.); also many species of varied heights and colours, reds, roses, pinks, lavenders, whites. Cover plants with cloches in winter if severe frosts likely. Raise new plants from cuttings in late summer and overwinter in a cold frame.

Euphorbia, crown of thorns

Polygonatum multiflorum
(Solomon's seal)
Arching stems set with oblong
pointed leaves. Flowers small, white
and narrowly tubular, borne singly, in
pairs or trebles along the entire length
of the underside of the stem. Spreads
by means of underground stems.
Any soil, thrives in limy. Best in
light shade where the leaves develop
well.
Raise new plants by dividing the
rootstock in autumn and planting out
rooted pieces 9–12 inches (23–30 cm.)
apart.

Tolmiea menziesii (pig-a-back plant)
Curious maple-shaped green leaves
produce baby plants from their centres.
Slender sprays of greenish flowers
appear in summer.
Ordinary soil, excellent for carpeting
in light shade beneath trees, or growing
as a pot plant in unheated conservatory.
Increase by removing sturdy plantlets
from leaf centres and potting them on
in small pots of rich gritty soil.

Shrubs

Aucuba (spotted laurel)
Rounded bush of evergreen leaves and
striking marble-sized berries in
autumn and winter. Species and forms:
A. japonica (male or female) glossy
spear-shaped leaves, scarlet fruits;
grow both sexes for fruiting.
'Crotonoides', mottled gold leaves;
'Fructu-albo', handsome leaves,
yellowish berries. Thrives in shade or
semi-shade, ordinary soil. Does well in
smoky atmosphere. Water freely in
summer, less in winter. Feed
fortnightly to encourage sturdy
growth in summer.
Raise plants from seed or cuttings.

Berberis (barberry)
Upright or spreading, deciduous or
evergreen bushes grown for their
spring flowers, autumn fruits and
autumn-tinted leaves. Stems and
leaves are spiny. Evergreen varieties:
B. linearifolia, orange flowers;
B. verruculosa, dark green leaves, pale
yellow flowers. Deciduous varieties:
B. thunbergii, red fruits; *B.t.* 'Aurea',
striking golden leaves; *B. wilsonae*,
golden yellow flowers, bright red
fruits, autumn-tinted foliage.
Ordinary soil, sun or shade. Water
freely in summer, hardly at all in
winter, but make sure soil stays damp.
Feed fortnightly if growth poor,
otherwise, not necessary.
Raise plants from seeds or cuttings.

Camellia
Glossy-leaved evergreen shrubs
(tender in coldest parts of North
America) with single, semi-double or
fully double flowers in many colours
including pink, white, scarlet and
blotched pink and white. Winter and
spring-flowering, acid soil essential or
leaves turn yellow and growth is poor.
Varieties of *C. japonica*: 'Adolphe
Audusson', crimson-scarlet; 'Gloire de
Nantes', rose-pink; 'Mathotiana Alba',
large white.
Feed with sequestered iron at regular
intervals through spring and summer
to induce strong healthy foliage.
Water freely, semi-shade.
Raise new plants from leaf bud
cuttings.

Caryopteris (blue spiraea)
Low spreading edging shrub with
spires of blue flowers in late summer.
Leaves silvery grey, aromatic. Sun or
semi-shade. Ordinary soil. Deciduous.
Varieties: 'Heavenly Blue', rich blue,
free flowering.
Water freely in summer, feed
fortnightly and water sparingly in
winter.
Pruning: cut back flowered shoots in
March to encourage strong new
growth from the base.
Raise new plants from cuttings.

Chamaecyparis (false cypress)
Evergreen conifer with upright or
rounded habit, with blue-green,
silvery, golden or grass-green foliage.
Grows best in acid soil though
tolerates ordinary soil.
Sun or shade. Golden variegated kinds
do best in sun.

Varieties: very numerous, especially of
C. obtusa and *C. pisifera*. Vary greatly
in size, shape, type of foliage and
colour. All grow slowly in tubs or
pots and need watering frequently in
summer, less in winter. Ideally feed
fortnightly throughout the summer.
Clip to shape in spring if shoots get
straggly.
Raise new plants from cuttings.

Choisya ternata (Mexican orange)
Glossy-leaved evergreen with bunches
of small cup-shaped, white, richly-
scented flowers in spring and
intermittently throughout the summer
and autumn. Ordinary soil in sun or
semi-shade, even dense shade.
Water freely in dry spells. Feed
fortnightly throughout the summer if
growth needs spurring along.
Raise new plants from cuttings.

Cistus (rock rose)
Large open flowers in white, red or
pink, often maroon blotched at the
base of petals: May to October. Ideal
for hot dry situations. Full sun,
ordinary soil with added peat.
Evergreen shrub with rounded or
spreading habit. Water freely in dry
spells, feed fortnightly if growth poor.
Varieties: *C. x corbariensis*, white;
C. x cyprius, white, blotched maroon;
'Silver Pink', silvery pink;
C. x purpureus, rosy crimson.
Raise new plants from seeds or
cuttings.

Clematis
Twining climber with mostly open
flat-petalled (sepalled) blooms in a
range of colours from white through
pink, red, blue, violet and purple.
There are even some yellow-flowered
kinds. Grow best with their roots in
the shade and shoots in the sun.
Deciduous and a few evergreen sorts.
Thrive in limy soil, though grow well
in most soils that drain freely and
have adequate plant foods.
Varieties: essentially there are the
large flowered hybrids such as purple
'Jackmanii', red and magenta 'Ernest
Markham', and bluish 'Mrs
Cholmondeley', and the species such
as *C. alpina*, blue with white stamens,
white *C. montana*, pink *C. montana*
'Tetrarose' and yellow *C. orientalis*.
Water freely throughout the summer,
less in winter. Feed fortnightly when
strong growth is made in spring and
early summer.

Raise new plants from layers, cuttings or seed. Prune by either cutting back previous year's growth to 2 feet (60 cm.) off the ground each February or early March, or simply shorten flowered shoots to within a few inches of the main upright branching system. Pruning given depends on variety.

Cotoneaster
Deciduous and evergreen kinds. Upright, rounded, spreading or ground covering shrubs with attractive leaves and berries. Sun or shade.
Varieties: accommodating evergreen kinds include ground-hugging, red-berried, glossy-leaved *C. dammeri*, sulphur-yellow-berried *C. rothschildianus* and handsome white-flowered, red-berried *C. lacteus*. Deciduous kinds are the herringbone cotoneaster, *C. horizontalis*, with masses of orange red berries on wiry flattened branches, perfect for growing close to a wall, and *C.* 'Hybridus Pendulus', a weeping variety usually grown as a standard.
Keep the soil moist in summer, less so in winter. Feed fortnightly if growth slow.
Raise new plants from cuttings or seeds.

Escallonia
Evergreen shrub with upright or spreading habit. Clusters of pink, red or white flowers borne along shoot tips in summer.
Varieties: 'Pride of Donard', rich red flowers in May; 'Iveyi', white flowers; 'Donard Seedling', apple-blossom pink.
Ordinary soil in full sun or light shade. Water freely in summer, less in winter. Feed to encourage sturdy growth.
Raise new plants from cuttings or layers.

Euonymus (spindle berry)
Attractive for its brilliant red autumn tinted leaves, coral-pink fruits and green variegated leaves. Sun or deep shade. Evergreen or deciduous.
Varieties: *E. alatus* is small roundish shrub with winged stems and bright autumn-tinted foliage; *E. europaeus* 'Red Cascade' is grown for its masses of large fruits; *E. fortunei* 'Emerald Gold' makes good ground cover with leaves margined with gold. Water freely in dry spells. No feeding necessary unless growth poor. All

forms of *E. fortunei* also excellent for training over walls provided suitable supports are erected.
Increase from layers, seeds, or cuttings.

Forsythia (golden bellflower)
Golden tubular starry flowers in spring. Bushes rounded and vigorous; cascading shoots in *F. suspensa*, which also makes a fine wall shrub. Varieties include: 'Lynwood', most free flowering; 'Beatrix Farrand', largest blooming variety; 'Arnold Dwarf', ideal for small tubs or window boxes. Ordinary soil. No feeding necessary, water freely in dry spells. Sun or semi-shade.
Raise new plants from layers or cuttings.

Hebe
Hardy, semi-hardy and tender, upright or spreading, evergreen, with mostly glossy leaves and cone-shaped flowers throughout the summer and autumn.
Varieties: *H. x andersonii* 'Variegata', with waxy, creamy leaves and lavender flowers; 'La Séduisante', plum purple flowers with reddish green leaves; 'Carl Teschner' dwarf, ideal for rock gardens, violet-blue flower sprays; *H. pagei*, grey-blue silvery leaves, white flowers, excellent for ground cover.
Sun or shade, normal soil. Water to keep roots moist in dry spells, hardly at all in winter.
Raise new plants from cuttings or layers.
No pruning needed apart from removing straggly shoots in early spring to keep bush shapely.

Hedera (English ivy)
Self-clinging evergreen climber. Ideal for sun, shade or deep shade. Leaves palmate or arrow-shaped, green or variegated.
Types: very numerous, large, small, all shapes, green and variegated.
Normal soil, water freely in dry spells. Feed only if growth poor. No pruning necessary apart from cutting back unwanted shoots in early spring.
Increase from layers or cuttings.

Hydrangea
Deciduous bushes or self-clinging climber. Mostly hardy. The lace caps have flattened blooms of fertile florets surrounded by sterile florets; the mopheads (hortensias) have roughly globe-shaped blooms of sterile florets.

Flowers lilac or reddish in neutral or limy soils, violet or blue in acid soils. Add hydrangea blueing powder to the root area to change red or lilac flowered varieties into blue-flowered specimens. Blooms in summer.
Varieties: 'Altona', red; 'Mariesii', pale rose or blue; 'Grayswood', violet purple and white, flushed red.
The one climbing hydrangea, *H. petiolaris*, has white flower discs in early summer and sticks to rough surfaces by means of stem roots, like an ivy.
Water whenever the soil is dry as hydrangeas need ample moisture to produce luxuriant leaves and fine flowers. Feed fortnightly throughout the summer. Plant in light shade. Prune in late spring, thinning out dead or weak shoots from centre of bush and cutting back faded flowers to healthy buds just below the blooms.
Raise new plants from layers or cuttings.

Hypericum (St John's Wort)
Starry or cup-shaped yellow flowers on upright or spreading shoots. Deciduous and evergreen.
Species and varieties: *H. calycinum*, large blooms with pronounced boss of yellow stamens; 'Hidcote', massed yellow flowers on rounded bush; *H. elatum* 'Elstead', grown for its salmon-red berry clusters and yellow flowers.
Ordinary soil. No feeding necessary, but water freely in dry spells.
Prune *H. calycinum* back hard in March to induce strong new growth from the base. 'Hidcote' and *H. elatum* should have their side shoots shortened to within a few inches of the older shoots in spring.
Raise new plants from seed or cuttings. Grow plants in good light or light shade. Blooms in summer and early autumn.

(above) *Mahonia aquifolium*

(left) *Prunus subhirtella* 'Pendula'

(right) *Clematis* 'King George'

Jasminum (jasmine)
Deciduous wall shrubs with scented
tubular flowers, for mild climates.
Species: *J. nudiflorum*, with bright
golden yellow flowers in winter; *J.
officinale*, with pure white flowers on
twining shoots, in summer.
Ordinary soil. No feeding necessary
unless growth is slow. Water freely
when soil dry in summer. *J. officinale*
grows best in full light, but *J.
nudiflorum* does not mind light shade.
Raise new plants from cuttings.
Pruning: shorten flowered shoots of
J. nudiflorum to within 2–3 inches
(5–7·5 cm.) of the main framework;
simply thin out stems of *J. officinale*;
no cutting back of flowered shoots
necessary.

Kerria (Jew's mallow)
Rounded bush with single or double
orange-yellow flowers on shoots set

with green or silvery variegated foliage. Blooms in April and May. Varieties: *K. japonica* 'Picta', silvery green leaves; *K. j.* 'Pleniflora', double flowers. Ordinary soil. This is a very hardy shrub and tolerates cold winds, shade and drought with little sign of discomfort. Looks well against a wall, too. Water freely through the summer, less so in winter. Feed only if growth is slow.
Prune flowered shoots back to strong new growth.
Raise new plants from cuttings or division of the rootstock.

Laurus nobilis (sweet bay, bay laurel)
Dark green spear-shaped leaves, small white flowers in spring. Leaves used in flavouring many dishes.
Makes a rounded bush if grown naturally, but often clipped to form a pyramid or standard with a ball head. Sheltered position in good light, not fully hardy. Ordinary soil. Water freely in summer, less in winter. No feeding required unless growth slow. Trim to shape in summer. No other pruning necessary.
Raise plants from cuttings.

Lavandula (lavender)
Evergreen rounded shrub with greyish silvery leaves and sweetly scented. Low growing. Flowers in summer. Varieties: *L.* 'Hidcote', deep violet-blue.
Best in well-drained soil in full sun. Does not mind long periods of drought. Water freely in summer or whenever the soil is dry. Feed fortnightly if growth poor.
Raise new plants from cuttings. Trim off flowered shoots in late summer; cut back old growth if straggly, in late spring.

Lonicera (shrubby and climbing honeysuckle)
Shrubby: *L. tatarica* most common, large, red-berried.
Climbing forms: semi-evergreen or evergreen – *L. japonica halliana*, creamy yellow flowers all summer. Deciduous: *L. periclymenum* 'Belgica', flowers with peaches and cream tints in early summer; *L. periclymenum* 'Serotina', creamy white, suffused purple flowers in summer and late summer; *L. heckrotii*, red and yellow flowers. The climbers twine their shoots round a supporting framework. Water and feed

regularly as climbing forms have extensive root system and can quickly deplete a tub of soil of its plant foods. Pruning: cut out old or weakly shoots on both climbing and shrubby sorts after flowering.
Raise new plants from layers or cuttings.

Mahonia
Evergreen sculptured shrub with statuesque leaves and yellow flowers in winter.
Varieties: *M. aquifolium*, creeping habit with bunches of bright yellow flowers followed by blue-black berries – late winter; *M. bealei*, larger, coarser, with larger leaves; 'Charity', probably the finest upright form with large stiff pinnate leaves and stems topped by pendulous flower sprays. Ordinary soil, sun or deep shade. No feeding necessary unless growth slow. Water well in summer, hardly at all in winter. Leaves suffer from wind burn in exposed places.
No pruning required, apart from cutting back *M. aquifolium* fairly hard if shoots become straggly.
Increase plants from seeds or cuttings.

Parthenocissus (Virginia creeper)
Self-clinging climber grown for its magnificent autumn-tinted leaves. Species: *P. henryana*, variegated white and pink palmate leaves; *P. quinquefolia* (true Virginia creeper), palmate leaves that take on brilliant scarlet hues in autumn.
Sun or shade. Ordinary soil. No feeding required.
No pruning necessary but cut back unwanted shoots in summer.
Raise new plants from cuttings.

Passiflora (passion flower)
Semi-evergreen climber with striking creamy white and blue flowers in summer.
Varieties: *P. caerulea*, flowers as above, and 'Constance Elliott', white. Thrives in sheltered, sunny position away from cold winds.
Ordinary soil. Water well in summer, less in winter. Feed fortnightly while flowers forming.
Prune side shoots back to 6 inches (15 cm.) of the main framework in early spring.
Raise new plants from layers or cuttings.

Pernettya
Ground hugging shrub with small

pointed leaves, tiny white flowers and highly attractive marble-sized berries in white, pink, mauve or scarlet. Winter decoration.
To get berries have one male plant together with several females. Varieties: *P. mucronata* 'Bell's Seedling', red berries; *P. mucronata* 'Alba', white berries.
Grow plants in peaty soil free from lime. Water freely in summer, less in winter, sun or shade, mild climate. No pruning necessary.
Raise plants from cuttings or layers.

Philadelphus (mock orange)
Upright or rounded shrub from 3 to 12 feet (0·9–3·7 m.) high, depending upon variety. Pure white, single or double, often maroon-blotched flowers borne freely along arching stems in mid-summer. Sun or light shade. Ordinary soil.
Varieties: 'Beauclerk', large white, cerise throated blooms; *P. coronarius* 'Aureus', white flowers, golden leaves; *P. microphyllus*, white flowers. *P. grandiflorus*, tallest sort with scentless flowers, often used for flower arranging as the sweet peppery scent of other varieties can cause irritation of eyes and nose.
Pruning: remove some of the older stems when the flowers fade. Retain young growth for flowering the following year.

Prunus (flowering cherries, plums, almonds, peaches)
Large family of deciduous trees and shrubs which flower mostly in spring. Some have brilliant autumn-tinted leaves. Branches are hung with blossom. Best in full sun; ordinary soil, with or without lime.

Varieties: (ornamental almond), *P. tenella* 'Firehill', dwarf habit, bright red flowers on every branch. Ornamental cherries: *P.* 'Amanogawa', pillar of pink flowers, narrow upright growth, ideal for confined spaces; *P. subhirtella* 'Autumnalis', white winter flowering; *P.* 'Okame', small tree with rosy pink flowers.

No pruning necessary, but should a branch need taking out, do this in late summer to reduce risk of attack by silver leaf disease.

Keep the soil moist in dry spells, feed if growth poor, otherwise not necessary.

Raise new plants by grafting varieties on to vigorous stocks; also by cuttings.

Pyracantha (firethorn)
Evergreen shrub. Grow as a specimen in the open, or against a wall or fence. Masses of foamy white flowers in early summer followed by clusters of berries in autumn and winter. Branches spiny.

Species and varieties: *P. angustifolia*, orange-red berries; *P. atalantioides*, red berries; *P. rogersiana* (syn. *P. crenulata rogersiana*) 'Flava', yellow berries.

Water freely throughout dry spells in summer. Feed fortnightly if growth slow.

Clip wall-trained shrubs with shears in early summer.

Raise new plants from cuttings.

Ribes (flowering currant)
Deciduous shrub draped with clusters of flowers in early spring. Makes a roundish bush. Ideal for deep shade or full sun. Ordinary soil.

Varieties: *R. sanguineum* 'King Edward VII', intense crimson; 'Pulborough Scarlet', deep red; 'Praecox', pink.

No feeding necessary. Water freely in dry spells. Shorten back old non-flowering shoots to near ground level in spring.

Raise new plants from cuttings.

Rosa (rose)
Single or double flowers borne on miniature, low growing, medium or large bushes. Deciduous, ordinary soil, sun or light shade. Climbing kinds also have single or double flowers.

Species: *Rosa rugosa* 'Frau Dagmar Hastrup', single pink flowers followed by rounded bright red tomato-sized hips.

Climbing species: *Rosa filipes*, vigorous, greyish green leaves, huge clusters of white flowers.

Old-fashioned roses: 'La Reine Victoria', double pink cup-like blooms; 'Mme Hardy', flattish pure white flowers.

Hybrid tea roses: 'Colour Wonder', orange salmon; 'Grandpa Dickson', creamy yellow pink-edged flowers; (North America: 'Mirandy', velvety wine-red; 'Eclipse', chrome-yellow).

Floribundas: 'Blessings', coral pink; 'Allgold', yellow; 'Fashion', coral peach; (North America: 'Fire King').

Climbers: 'Golden Showers', yellow.

Ramblers: 'Dorothy Perkins', bluish pink flowers.

Miniatures: 'Baby Masquerade', flame and gold; 'Coralin', orange and pink; 'Cinderella', white; (North America: 'Crimson Gem').

Pruning: aim at keeping in as much young wood as possible. Cut away bare lengths of non-flowering wood and keep the centres of bush roses well thinned. Remove faded flowers and stems of rambler roses completely, tying in new growths to flowers the following year. Leave the species roses and most of the old-fashioned kinds well alone, apart from keeping them shapely. Carry out all pruning in mid-February, early March or before growth begins in spring.

Raise new plants from cuttings or budding varieties on to appropriate stocks.

Rosmarinus (rosemary)
Aromatic evergreen with narrow leaves and upright spikes of flower. Ideal for dry, windy spots and hot sunny areas. Useful culinary herb.

Varieties: *R. officinalis*, light blue; *R. o.* 'Albus', white flowers.

Ordinary soil in sun or shade. Keep the soil moist in dry spells, though plant can tolerate long periods without water.

Pruning not required. No feeding necessary unless growth poor.

Spiraea
Deciduous shrubs with low rounded habit or arching stems. Starry flowers borne in flattened heads or tapering plumes. Mostly spring flowering.

Species and varieties: *S. thunbergii*, white clusters of bloom; *S. menziesii*, bright rosy pink flower cones in summer; *S. bullata*, low growing, ideal for rock gardens, crimson flowers in umbrella heads; *S. x bumalda* 'Anthony Waterer', crimson flowers.

Sun or deep shade, normal soil. Water freely in summer. Feed only if growth is weak.

Prune back flowered shoots of *S. x bumalda* in February or March. Prune *S. menziesii* after flowering – simply cut back flowered stems to strong buds below.

Raise new plants from cuttings and layers.

Syringa (lilac)
Upright deciduous shrubs with imposing spires of bloom in late spring and early summer. Single or double flowers. *Syringa palibiniana*, dwarf kind, ideal for containers.

Large varieties: 'Esther Staley', clear pink; 'Primrose', creamy yellow; 'Charles Joly', dark red; 'Edith Cavell', white.

Sun or semi-shade, ordinary soil. Water freely in summer, feed only if shoot growth weakly.

Prune off faded flowers in summer. Raise new plants from cuttings or grafting varieties on to stock plants.

Tamarix (tamarisk)
Feathery rose-pink flowers borne in mid-summer among bright green ferny leaves. Height: 9–12 feet (2·7–3·7 m.). Full sun. Deciduous. Ordinary soil but hates lime.

Varieties: *T. parviflora*, deep pink flowers; *T. pentandra* 'rubra', rose-red

flowers; *T. tetrandra*, pink flower plumes borne on shoots produced the previous year.
Pruning: keep bush shapely by cutting back around half of the previous season's shoots. Deal with *T. pentandra* from early autumn to late winter and *T. tetrandra* when the flowers fade.
Raise new plants from cuttings in October.

Vitis (ornamental vine)
Vigorous climber ascending by means of clinging tendrils. Can grow to 60 feet (18 m.) or more in favoured situations. Deciduous, ordinary soil, sun or light shade. Perfect for covering walls, fences, arbours, trees or pergolas.
Species and varieties: *V. coignetiae*, the Japanese crimson glory vine. Large heart-shaped leaves of striking appearance which turn scarlet and orange in autumn; *V. vinifera* 'Purpurea', handsome claret-coloured vine-shaped leaves, deeply lobed, colouring well in autumn.
Prune out congested shoots in summer. Encourage new growth to fill allotted area.
Raise new plants from stem cuttings in November, but increase *V. coignetiae* by layering stems.

Weigela (syn. *Diervilla*)
Rounded shrub with arching branches bearing sprays of foxglove-shaped flowers in spring and early summer. Leaves green or variegated. Height: 6–8 feet (1·8–2·4 m.).
Ordinary soil in sun or light shade. Varieties: *W. florida* 'Foliis Purpureis', purple-hued leaves, rosy purple blooms; *W. florida* 'Variegata', leaves margined white, pink flowers; *W. middendorffiana*, large sulphur-yellow flowers.
Pruning: shorten flowered stems and some older shoots back to ground level when the flowers fade. Aim at keeping young free-flowering growth.

Wistaria
Vigorous twining climber with handsome pinnate leaves and long racemes of bloom in spring. Deciduous, ordinary soil, full sun. Varieties: *W. floribunda* 'Alba', long white flower clusters; *W. sinensis*, lavender-blue flowers.
Pruning: shorten all side shoots back to 2–3 buds from the base of the previous year's growth in late winter, early spring.
Raise new plants from seeds, layers or cuttings.

Berberis

Care of Plants

❧ Watering ❧

One of the disadvantages of gardening in the city is that only too often the gardens or patios are very hot in summer and plants tend to dry out quickly.

If suitable materials can be obtained – spent hops, peat, or even sawdust – a layer 1–2 inches (2·5–5 cm.) deep over the soil, whether in borders, tubs or window boxes, helps to retain moisture and reduce the frequency of watering. It also helps to suppress weeds which in themselves rob the plants of moisture.

It is well worth while going to the expense of installing an outside water tap or faucet. Some water authorities object to the installation of permanent sprinklers or watering devices, such as punctured hose spray lines, if these are in contact with the soil. These objections can often be overcome if a non-return valve is fitted into the system.

There are now many different types of sprinkler for watering large or small areas, and there are even water- and electric-operated timing devices which can be set to apply water for given periods.

You can tailor-fit a garden for water by laying a plastic main or pipe down one side if it is a rectangular garden, or round several sides if it is of irregular shape. Then fittings, rather like electric light sockets, are fitted at intervals in the main. A similar but 'male' plug is then fitted to a short length of hose pipe, at the other end of which is a sprinkler or a length of spray line.

When you wish to water a given part of the garden you just 'plug into the main'. With several outlets, it is only necessary to have a short, easily carried length of hose connecting the main or supply pipe to the sprinkler, and it is just moved round the garden as required.

If a series of irregular beds or containers of various sizes have to be watered, it is possible to connect them all to the water main by means of a length of semi-rigid plastic pipe. Then above the bed or container, holes are punctured or drilled in the pipe in sufficient number to water the bed in a reasonable time. If water is required more quickly you just make some more holes. Again, if a hole should become bunged up for any reason, it is simple enough to puncture another one. A simple tool for making the holes is a bradawl filed down to about the thickness of a gramophone needle.

There are, of sourse, the sub-irrigation kits originally designed for use on greenhouse benches, which can be used to water plants in pots outdoors. Basically these consist of shallow trays connected, if more than one tray is used, by a plastic tube. The trays are filled with sand and then connected by another tube to a small tank or cistern which is filled with water. This keeps the sand in the trays wet and pot plants are stood on the sand. The roots draw up moisture as they require it. The cistern may be filled as required by means of a hose pipe, but it may be connected to the mains supply and fitted with a ball valve. The sand trays will thus be always kept moist.

Such equipment, of course, may be used to keep house plants watered while the owner is away, provided there is room to set it up although those with an octopus-like arrangement of tiny tubes are better for such a purpose. These self-watering trays may even be used on a balcony or on the floor of a kitchen, to keep the plants watered when the owner is on holiday.

91

Storing geraniums

✤ Overwintering Plants ✤

In days gone by, when plants and bulbs were relatively cheap, the city gardener was happy enough to buy new bedding plants every year. Now it is important to preserve certain of our bedding plants from year to year.

Ideally, bulbs such as daffodils, tulips and hyacinths grown in containers should be allowed to die down naturally; then the top growth is removed, the bulbs cleaned up, dried off and kept in a cool dry place for replanting in the autumn. This means that you need spare boxes, or inner containers, which can be put in some out-of-the-way corner and watered until the foliage begins to wither naturally. Or better still, if you have an odd corner in the garden or in a friend's garden, the bulbs can be laid in a trench, covered up to half the length of their stems with soil and dried off gradually.

The summer flowers that we should try to lift and preserve through the winter are geraniums, fuchsias, dahlias, gladioli and begonias.

Before frosts arrive in the autumn, lift the geranium plants, trim back the roots, cut the stems down to about 8 inches (20 cm.) long and pack the plants fairly close together in a large pot or box. Pack them in sandy soil, or peat and keep this just slightly moist all winter. In spring pot the plants separately, or plant out when frost danger is over. Treat fuchsias similarly.

With dahlias wait until the foliage has been blackened by frost. Cut the plants down to 12 inches (30 cm.) above ground. Lift the roots carefully. Stand them upside down in a frost free place for 10–12 days. Then put them in boxes and cover the tubers with peat but do not cover the 'crown' of the plant – the point on the stem to which the tubers are attached. It is from this point that new shoots will appear next year and it is important that no rotting takes place here. Keep the peat just moist all winter, and store the plants in a frost free place. Divide into separate pieces each with a tuber and a live growing shoot and replant the tubers in late April; see that there is 6 inches (15 cm.) of soil over the crown of the plant.

Lift gladiolus plants as soon as they have finished flowering. Cut the stems to about 3·4 inches (7·5–10 cm.) above the corms. Store the corms in a single layer in trays in a frost free place.

Lift tuberous begonias before the onset of frost. Put them in a tray or box and allow the stems to wither naturally. Then break them away from the tubers and store these, covered with peat, in trays in a frost free place. In early spring start them into growth by moistening the peat, and plant them in pots or out again when danger of frost is passed.

✤ Frames and Cloches ✤

If there is no space for a greenhouse or a home extension, there may be room for a frame and this can be a great asset. It can be used to raise seedlings and root cuttings and in summer to grow 1 or 2 cucumber plants.

If it is fitted with an electric soil warming cable buried in sand, it is even more useful as seeds may be sown several weeks earlier, and it may be used to grow lettuces and early carrots in the winter, and early spring.

Even more valuable is a frame fitted with both soil and air warming cables. The air warming cables are fitted by special clips to the inside of the frame. With thermostatic control the frame may be kept free of frost, and running costs are not high. It may be powered from a power socket in the house.

Such a frame may be set up on a patio or small terrace at the back of the house, say in late September, and used for overwintering geraniums and other tender plants if the climate is not too severe. In the spring it could be used to raise seedlings of tender annuals, tomatoes and sweet corn plants for planting out. Then, say at the end of May, it may be disconnected and the

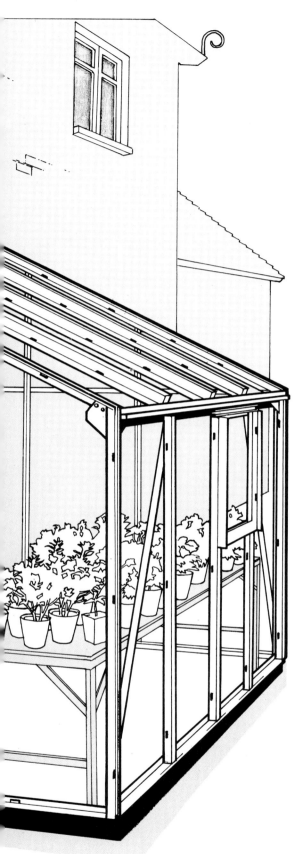

frame stood on end, covered with a sheet of plastic, to make more room.

If there is no space for a frame, or you do not want to go to that expense, a few glass or plastic cloches are an excellent investment. Not only will they permit the sowing of tender plants like sweet corn, French and runner beans, and marrows in late April, ahead of season, but also planting of these in early May if they have been bought in or raised indoors or in a heated greenhouse.

Cloches also hasten the growth of peas, broad beans, lettuces and carrots sown under them in late February or March. With lettuces, the cloches give protection against damage by birds.

The Greenhouse and Frames

For anyone who enjoys growing plants, a conservatory, a home extension with glass walls, however small, or a small greenhouse can be a great joy. Such a structure enables you to work with the plants at any time – after dark if need be, and in the winter when there is little to do in a small garden.

Even more rewarding, however, are the benefits such glass protection can provide in the way of better plants and the saving of money.

There are many pot plants which can do a turn in the home for a few weeks, but then need to be given a period of convalescence in a greenhouse with more congenial conditions of light and humidity.

Many plants may be propagated by cuttings, or raised from seed in a greenhouse or conservatory, saving a considerable outlay at the florists. Plants for tubs, window boxes, beds or borders can be propagated, and the tender plants such as geraniums and fuchsias overwintered without difficulty.

By a careful choice of plants you can have flowers in the greenhouse all the year round and, of course, plenty of foliage plants. You can also grow a grape vine, or tomatoes, cucumbers and salad plants in a greenhouse.

While some people prefer wooden greenhouses, the modern trend is towards aluminium, either as a lean-to or as a free-standing house. They used to be much more expensive than wooden houses, but now, as wood is so expensive, they are as cheap as a really good quality wooden house. They need no maintenance and of course last for many years.

While a cold greenhouse or conservatory is better than no greenhouse, one that is equipped to keep the minimum night temperature at 7–10°C. (45–50°F.) is infinitely more valuable. A cold house may be used to push bulbs and other hardy flowers to bloom a little earlier than they would outdoors. But a heated house permits a vast variety of plants to be grown. The heat may be provided by paraffin, kerosene or gas or bottle-gas heaters, by electric heaters, or as an extension of a central heating system.

Apart from enhancing the pleasure of gardening, a greenhouse can effect savings if you usually buy pot plants, cut flowers or bedding plants.

A greenhouse should be sited to obtain most of the available sunlight and is best if its long side faces south, south west or west.

Useful Equipment

If there are beds and borders to be dug over, a spade and a fork are necessary. For small areas a small spade or fork is all that is required.

A rake, a long handled hoe, a short handled or onion hoe, a trowel, and a small hand fork are also necessary. Secateurs or pruning shears will be required for pruning and cutting down woody or herbaceous plants.

Also very handy are a trug, plastic bucket or basket for gathering rubbish and some kind of incinerator for burning woody garden rubbish if outdoor burning is permitted in your area. Soft rubbish – leaves and stems of plants that are finished should be rotted down in a compost heap.

93

String and plastic covered wire which can be cut into short lengths for tying plants to stakes are essential; so is a small sprayer for applying insecticidal and fungicidal sprays. A watering can fitted with a fine rose is also a necessity, and if there is any paving to be kept clear of weeds, an old table fork bent over at right angles is useful.

❧ Pests and Diseases ❧

Let us dispose of diseases first because these are not so serious in most towns as in country districts. This is because the impurities in the atmosphere help to prevent the spread of diseases. However, these are the most common:

Black spot Affects roses, showing as black or purple spots; afterwards leaves yellow and fall prematurely. Spray with captan or maneb every two weeks after pruning. Burn or otherwise remove and destroy all prunings and fallen leaves and petals.

Mildew White powdery patches, affects roses, tomatoes, chrysanthemums and many other garden plants. Spray with a fungicide recommended for use on the affected plants immediately the disease is noticed. Another year apply preventive sprays *before* disease appears.

Peach leaf curl May affect almonds, apricots and peaches and nectarines. Leaves become swollen, puckered, red and distorted. Spray with lime sulphur or Bordeaux mixture in January or February, again a fortnight later. Spray also at leaf fall in the autumn.

Rust Many plants are affected by rust diseases, brown or black spots on the foliage. Roses, hollyhocks and many other flowers, and some vegetables are affected. Rusts are not easy to control. Burn all diseased foliage at the end of the season. Spray with a copper fungicide as soon as the disease is noticed, and repeat every 14 days.

Tomato blight This disease is similar to the blight that affects potatoes, and may affect outdoor tomatoes. Spray with a copper fungicide in early July, and repeat twice at 14-day intervals.

Apart from birds, cats and dogs which have been mentioned on p. 57, the following are the pests most commonly found in city gardens:

Aphis This group consists of green and black fly. Greenfly are found on roses, lilies, chrysanthemums and many other plants. Black fly are common on beans and dahlias. Spray with a suitable insecticide as soon as pests appear. Check plants once or twice a week, especially the underside of the leaves.

Caterpillars Many caterpillars – the larvae of butterflies and moths – attack ornamental plants, fruits and vegetables. Inspect plants once or twice a week, and spray with derris or any recommended insecticide immediately the pests are noticed, repeating the spray as advised by the manufacturers.

Earwigs These pests damage the blooms of dahlias, chrysanthemums, clematis and other plants. Keep the gound clear of fallen leaves and other rubbish under which they may hide, and dust on and around the plants with BHC or trichlorphon.

Leaf miners These caterpillars tunnel into the leaves of chrysanthemums and cause white 'mines' in the leaves. They seldom cause much damage, but in severe infestations spray with BHC or other recommended insecticide.

Slugs and snails Every garden suffers from these pests which can do untold damage to your seedlings and tender young shoots of delphiniums and other perennials. Keep the ground clear of fallen leaves and weeds under which slugs and snails can hide in the day time. Immediately their slimy trails are noticed put down metaldehyde slug bait, or water the ground and plants with liquid slug killer. Remove and destroy dead or moribund slugs each morning. Some may only be drugged and may recover.

94

Index

Acknowledgments

The author is grateful to Mr. John Negus for his assistance with the A-Z plant descriptions.
The publishers are grateful to the following people for their permission to reproduce the photographs in this book.
A-Z Botanical Collections Ltd: 26–27, 77, 90 Elli Beintema: 66–67 British Tourist Authority: 38 below Camera Press: 10, 22–23, 70 W. F. Davidson: 66 inset, 87 House Beautiful: 42–43 G. E. Hyde: 30, 43 right, 47, 63, 79, 82, 83, 86 above, 86 below W. McLaughlin: 62 below Picturepoint Ltd: 38 above, 39 H. Smith: 58, 59, 75 Spectrum Colour Library: 11, 31, 62 above Violet Stevenson: 14–15, 51 above, 71 Syndication International Ltd: 18–19 Linda Yang (The Terrace Gardener's Handbook): 50, 51 below
Illustrations by:
Barrington Barber: 16–17, 36–37, 44–45, 68–69; Andrew Farmer: 20, 21, 24, 25, 92–93; Vana Haggerty: 1, 29, 32, 33, 34, 48–49, 53, 76, 77, 80, 81, 84, 85, 88, 89; Rodney Shackell: 4–5, 8, 9, 28, 40–41, 74.